SONGS F

Songs for the Phoenix focuses on the spirit ... ,
within. It is, at the same time, a celebration of collective life and the
ideal mission of the divine Messenger. Highly charged with spiritual
intensity, yet also highly readable, these poems by award-winning
poet Michael Fitzgerald bring clarity out of complexity, purpose out of
chaos. *Songs for the Phoenix* includes a selection of poems published
previously and over one hundred and fifty new poems.

Michael Fitzgerald is the author of seven books of poetry, three books
of non-fiction, a National Book Award nominee, and the winner of
several awards. He has taught workshops and read his poems in
Europe, Canada and the United States. He has worked on projects for
Warner Brothers, the Smithsonian Institution, National Public
Radio, Ralph Nader's groups, the US Department of Energy,
Defenders of Wildlife, and the US Bahá'í National Center. He makes
his home in the Shenandoah Valley of Virginia.

BY THE SAME AUTHOR

Poetry

A Tree Like This
Living the Boundaries
New World Suite
God's Whimsy
Rhapsody
Planet Dreams
Windows
New Seeds
Spirit Suite
Night Songs

Nonfiction

The Creative Circle (ed.)
Short Takes
In Brief
Briefly Speaking

Michael Fitzgerald

Songs

for the

Phoenix

Selected Poems 1984–1994

GEORGE RONALD
OXFORD

George Ronald, Publisher
46 High Street, Kidlington, Oxford OX5 2DN

ISBN 0-85398-393-3
*A Cataloguing-in-Publication entry is available from
the British Library*

Credits and Acknowledgements

Some of these poems have appeared in the folllowing publications: *Cabletalk* with Barry Lee, the *Dan River Anthology*, *Oasis*, the *Association of Bahá'í Studies Journal* of Chile, *Voices Israel*, *Forum* (New Zealand), *Paideia*, the *Dreams Anthology*, Northwoods Press editions, and Rainbow's End books; and in the chapbooks *New Seeds, Night Songs* and *Spirit Suite*. Some have also appeared as Handworks Gallery Broadsides, in performance with Doc Holladay of the Kenton, Ellington, Gillespie and Woody Herman Bands, in performance with Dream Harvest, the multi-media group, and live and on tape with Seth Austen, acoustic guitar, courtesy Turquoise Records; and guitarist John Albertson, George Washington University. 'Vision Quest' was set to music by Patrick O'Shea, of the Washington Oratoria Society and the Shenandoah Conservatory of Music.

Many thanks are due to my editor, May Hofman, and to Wendi Momen, Larry Muller, and to my family. Thanks also to Howard Richards, Peace Studies, Earlham College; to Ron Santoni, Denison University; to Gil Klose, Economics, Earlham College; to the Iowa Writers Workshop; to Charles Wolcott, William Sears and David Ruhe; and to Roger White. Special thanks are also due to Elizabeth Fitzgerald for consultation and assistance with the manuscript, and to the estate of Virginia W. Merrill for funding.

NOTE TO THE READER

I sing these songs
from the vortex,
from the placeless urge,
from the drive to go on,

somehow to rise up
amid the late century chaos,
somehow to say "Yes!" —
yes to the future within the present,

yes, to Bahá, to singing,
yes to the inexorable drive towards peace

Contents

viii

I

From

A Tree Like This

"Follow your bliss."
Joseph Campbell

A Tree Like This

~~A perfect tree,~~
~~it is the universal Self, the One~~
totem. If there were no further reason
for this Tree's healing
it would be the substance of justice.
It comes of the readiness to see that war's
red river of semiotic blood, the verifiable
evidence of our demise, is the sense
of intensity at the heart of trees
broken open with savage blows at life itself.
It is a particular tree, the re-invention
of the paradisical, the idea of humanity
as "the leaves of one tree",* like the
capable and luminous in substantial form.
I am thinking of the credible,
the soaring lines of becoming,
the single point for the definition of eternity.

His roots, like the idea of a region
to the world, acquire their redolent reasons
of timelessness in the remembrance of Abraham
and the balm of Gilead. There, the crest
of ocean's waves are human highness
and the minor key of a Beethoven
grasps oppression in its place.
Then, the sound of innocence becomes
the wisping of the branches in the wind,
and the sight of this standard
in the garden itself
restores human intrinsic feeling.

* *Bahá'u'lláh*

A perfect tree,
like the idea of trees, or notes
in the mind of the first musician.
A measure of His human, actual form,
is the kindness of mothers,
and the patience of unenviable nature
in its glacial recovery from the hand
of human evil. I am working
on a feeling so praiseworthy that I will
offer it up at the mention
of this Tree, forty years hence
in my hopes of dying a good death.

The sky is His sable curve
in a cosmos as wide as things,
as plural as the first stone.
I have spent my life looking at trees
and have yet to see the furthest extent
of this Tree of Life. It is by the branches
of this Tree that I affirm the survival of
the human race in the nuclear age.
I am thinking of a cypress in Israel
as perfect as Buddha/as perfect as Christ.
Bahá'u'lláh, this Tree, the very reason
to reclaim religion in a time of Inquisitions/
the palatial heart I take to in my poverty/
the motive of languages/the Tree as primal Word/
a Tree like this.

Rare, the Giving

Rare, the giving
that leads, and lends a hand

to poets, prayers,
and promises of peace.
Rare, the friend
<u>sitting in the hull of the Ark</u>
<u>rowing side by side</u>
<u>with rebel oarsmen,</u>
staying them to the work
in a word, in a brilliant laugh.
Too high, the praise of the world,
too low, the antonym of paradise,
we, we, strive to see
in the dark time, the flash
of fireflies in the neon-countryside.
Knowing, unknowing,
flash to dark to flash,
stir to hear the peace-gift,
turn to dance the lift
of feet treading on the temple ground —
    when the totem is Sabean, Jew,
      Christian, Moslem,
      and the rosette of the Bahá'ís.

Rolling out the Order of Bahá'u'lláh,
rolling out, the Tongue of Grandeur
in the unity-tent
to cry out "Peace! Peace!"
and we see, hear, feel the peace, in a miracle
of light in history-dancing.
It is there.
It is likely candidate,
only horse
in the race
for oneness.

                We mount,
trepid, intrepid,
tried, tested,
purified, exalted,
stirred, girded,
torn in the wilderness,
in the quest
"to know and love God",
the Almighty Creator
of star-things
glittering, glistening
about our searcher-heads
in a galaxy of finding.
Weather the storm, ahead,
to the Bay of Akka.
Whether we last,
whether we make it
may not be so much,
so necessary —
the dance to light
in history-making,
this quest, this quest,
this must go on,
this, and to it
        we lift our feet
        on the temple-ground.

Chicago. Samoa.
Kampala. Sydney.
Home.

Or maybe Indiana-heart
where the temple
of being stays grounded, hidden

in the "number 9,
number 9".

It is oneness
phrases of rare, rare
giving of the friends
to poets, prayers
and promises of peace
in a justice-time
rising.

Crescendo of the Ark —
maintain.
Your home is the Ark-line, the archive,
the Assembly, the wood-grain
floor, the Word,
the road.

Lady, lay by,
I am coming home a desperado, a
seeker for the soul of Krishna,
in the image of the Ark-men,
men to earth-time,
rowing, relentless, heaving,
shots over the bridge,
into the dark night
of boundless light,
rowing.

Hospitals

The needle breaks the surface
in slow-soft precision
on a background of whole flesh.

I lean back to ponder
the mechanical love
as the nurse hits the hospital

bricks as soon as it is over.
Needle, bright and silver, out.
Projectile to the blood, gone.

I ease into sleep. Is it only
because I no longer hear her touch?
What ministry does the chemical perform?

Is it anywhere the potent medicine
of her dress, her arms touching me?
I am left. The window out onto the city
protects me from bleeding onto the floor.

II

"Christ" passes across some modern lips
like the metaphor of some idea
twice removed from the concept.

Still, the path to praises
traces down the one thing we know
for prayer — seeking the resonance of love —

This wintered Name and His living legacy
cross paths in the hospitals
where moments of human speaking –

despite denominations,
despite encrusted dogmas –
say what it is we all long for.

The cancer patient – terminal –
who writes her own funeral –
as a Celebration;

The psych ward where someone
who thought he was God
accepts a piece of his own humanity;

The chaplain who dies a little
with the patient by admitting
to being scared about – what next – himself.

III

The especially sick especially cherish hope.
It is their strange and vital medicine
when medicine falters.

Life and death side by side –
one, bustling nurses,
the tonic of visitors,

youthful rebellions and adult competencies;
the other, clamoring for your submission
with dubious promises of peace –

you choose the first sometimes
only because you must —
your soul, though worn, will have it no other way.

Even sophisticates may subscribe to
the power of positive thinking with their backs
up against their own mortality.

IV

We are all plagued by half-hidden secrets
between the gray sighs under the covers
as they wheel by another stretcher —

Compassion hides them with poor memory —
and a smile — our muscles rest in smiling
and regenerate with laughter;

Prayers may be answered in a quick death;
or jogging or whirlpools —
much less the tossing aside of crutches at the altar.

Healing of minds, hearts and bodies
is not the sole property of doctors or sects.
It is the conjunction of love and science.

I do not cross myself
except as a Hindu, Buddhist, Jew — Bahá'í —
who found Christ flat on my back.

V

Choose truth for love is its source
and the dominant note of the universe.
It will claim any situation of suffering

for its victory without regard to credentials.
The Christ legacy is lived out each time
we choose to overcome our smallness,

to realize the largesse of the Creator
of religions is available at each turn . . .
Quietly, I enter the semi-private room and bow down,

Quietly, I realize that it is not so much
I who choose, but Him who heard my cry
before I chose.

Men

Manage, we do. We look for problems to manage when they
aren't there. Too much time in the army when humanity was
a little boy-girl, learning to wield our regiments. It is

sneaking up on yourself to find that something sublime
has passed you by in the night and nowhere is there
a tell-tale sign except your grazed conscience.

I look out the window in Kittery Point, Maine, to see if
there's any wind, any sign of a female instinct left
in my soul or if it has been blotted out by too much

fiery rhetoric, too many sold-out bedside stories
where the whole human race is gathered between the two
of us to hear about Ben Hur and Alexander when Ruth

would do very well. For a day-long century one noon,
I wept over Israel to see her killing herself in the

war over Ishmael and Isaac, sprung from one seed. Men.
We manage to look like we're in charge when all the potatoes

in Ireland are gone, 1846, to drink and wenches.
Leave it to the Muses to cover, to care for the lost
women poets. For the men are weary of bearing their
side of the load too high, too close to the shoulder holster

to see that the sun is rising over Easter and Mary
Magdalene is there hiding in the rock. We are managing
a box of matches, a tinderbox able to ignite the human arteries

for giving out of need, the desperate response, at zero
hour, we are managing the button. We are managing our

graying temples, our squadrons and our legions of
career-minded, business-suited, time-in, time-out,
givers of endless 9 to 5. Our flex-time is our muscle-bending.

Our life is our loan to the debtor nations which
we must repay with forgiveness of our debt to them
with a credit line straight to Zimbabwe. It is the
hand up to Ariel; it is the Hill and the reception

where Nick, Susan and I discuss the World Bank, Gwendolyn
Brooks, Navaho, Dharma Bums, and tribal reunion. It is
our joining in our find, our release from armies to live, to live.

The Story Goes

The story goes
he is a timeless agent
beyond the future,
within the stars,
and over the sea
in a chariot.

They would have it
he is the Invisible
Free, the Connector
and Fire. But,

the coral in my over the horizon
sea-scape keeps naming
him shape-of-my-heart;
and the shells in the window
call him resonant stone.

The kinship of fly wheels
and the marlin's blue tail
makes me all that is wondering,
and the credo of sea scallops
vibrates
with the dust of his eons, the
rest of his trouble
over my doing
makes the in-dwelling house
of his timelessness
here.

Capturing a Vision

Because
you have come in view,
there surge a lake and waves,
the cusp and the apex peal
with an absolution and a promise
that wind will be at my back.

The freedom
of your embraces
new, rehearsed, known, affirmed,
quits me in the hollows of my perfect hands,
silence and a flowing fountain
comfort me until no longer
will the nearness nestle nor
the willow wisp.

O Untrammelled, Quicksilver
Friend, Fable in Sight, leave,
and be thou Gold! Stay,
and be thou Fire! Die
to Live and Come Thou Once
Forever!

Night

Night listens to the following day
like the ear of Eden,
knowing its imminent expulsion, low
to the ground and quiet;

if it forces the very issue
known as the break of day
it is because
things have never been worse.

The craven look it casts
towards its omnipresent brother Sun,
looks for its own dissimulation
to the court where it nods.
It is, in a word, a traitor and
a larcenous being who lives for itself.
Closer than any day, it is the
shadow of things that are.

Kings And Blond Boys Waking

Brace a boisterous blond boy to his face
Build a solemn city in your heart
Carry former days like ivory and the night
to the rose of waking's morning light, build

a structure, a Fane for all the world in new
redemptive hue and worlds of worlds,
and galaxies will shine therein for universes
find a union in such a force a'making.

Cedar, cypress, pine and glory
hyacinths and sweets, flowers in the desert
raking sky and lacing wounded zephyrs
with that Ancient tongue of Beauty, high! high!

When the Blessed Beauty reigns, the kings
redeem the time and earth shall be ordered, still, still.

Fine Lines

Does the architect in you thirst
for fine lines and complexity, elegantly
portrayed? Is there a quest in the garden
for the perfect drawing?

When my grandfather laid down his pen,
his father had been gone awhile, sketching sermons
over his son's shoulder for forty years.
The subject of generations precludes
excess of distinctions when
the chicken houses on the Massachusetts farms include

porticos, gables and the minister of twelve
hiding in the hayloft
with Chaucer or was it Dante?
I never leave home without a note pad and pen.

A Cul De Sac

A cul de sac
in a sea
of old ways crumbling;

I believe, then,
in the sea

which tosses
sea lions and
driftwood ashore.

I lie here, aching
to thrash mid-sea, to be more,

but the waves have cast me
out of their weather
and thraldom to paradise
has me bold, broken.

On The Day of Your Becoming

For a Friend

From a median point of the last compass
you took into the country,

the trees gave leaves and the sky wondered.
Interests became interests again

and theatre came to your ears with music.
Why became being and why not was your leader

in the 60s aura that never stopped living.
The simple resonance of your song clipped

the impossibility of the day into proportion
like the perfect hand of destiny sweeping

the weeds from your garden. Mixed, stirred,
penetrated, you became the person who could

guide a ship into a mined harbor, the man
who could turn his back on parallel fifths

and learn the becoming of seeing oneness
in a javanese gamelan. From there, dare I,

you leapt in the spring of the whole universe
with ecstasy like the spirit. It was, it was.

There in the heart of your afterthoughts, the jasmine,
you lingered like sage, parceled out for your days,

until clover became a mine for your digging.
The ferreting, undone diversity of it left you spinning,

but the ferocity of its reason came into you like fire.
It was to − not a not to − it is the person you are,

you have given yourself to the wisdom you have found
and back in New Hampshire there is a lake and pines.

From a New Delhi Journal

A surrounding fall in Charlottesville, Virginia,
the raided roses, the burnt memory
of Jefferson passes through our fingers
like so many tea leaves to tell by.

A Chinese professor has arrived
and we speak of the bull, the old,
the drive to build, to civilize.
The cafe where we speak lies
a few paces from the rotunda,
the center, here.

The coffee, Columbia Supremo,
arrives, breaking our talks as flies linger,
split the veneration, the possibility.
He nods at the door as
a group of robed priets of medicine
cast shadows in the light.

A Confucian, he mentions the operation
his wife has had. With best wishes, we depart.
It is never more. It is seldom less. We drive
to his apartment and I wave,
savoring his smile.

II

The long drive to Winchester,
I listen to the mainstream jazz station
Ellington, Fitzgerald, Hubbard;
Marvin Holliday, an Ellington man,
has left for a tour
a month after his wedding.
He must be fifty-six by now,
graying, still thin, his sax,
pitched like rain
in a Shenandoah wind.
I sense there is something more,
a Sunrise, another Song.

III

The tape player is broken, the backseat
piled with books, a towel, a trumpet
cased like an ivory tusk.
The man I was is still; the radio

dimly plans an Arlo Guthrie tune,
a cowboy song and I am going
fishing. The sweat of the day
is an Irishman working.

IV

The heavy smoke from
Rugby Road tells a half-hour story
of unrepentant rage and
ambition sated. The languor of youth
and the copies of the tarot tossed.
There is a time for all of this.

V

New Delhi lifts a new lotus,
a temple I have never known.
The timeless shadow of the gift is given.
Temperate and beautiful, there is
in this unveiling a crown such as gathers
to commemorate a temple. The stone has been
overturned and no one dares sigh
or loose an idle world.
There is a singleness;
     the point of reflection
     is found; the streets recoil.
     An interest, a making, the Victory.
     It is nevertheless, a lotus, looming and given,
     so we must go.

VI

The Trumpets. There are Trumpets.
The door is opening "as wide as heaven and earth".

The cost is everything
and the Rose listens to our prayers.

The home in the poor, the casting away of riches.
the life on the road, it is never so given.
We never stay; we die to live.
There is a sitar. There are hymns and chants.
A Book. The signs upon miracles dancing.
The epiphany of giving twice.
"Never and always." Here,
and in New Delhi.

God's Archers

For Boynton Merrill, author of Arrows of Light, and my grandfather.

God's archers
are the angels
I respect —

they clarify space and time
with the precision
of "arrows and light" —

the direction of living
is the war with oneself —
the battle of samsara, illusion —
the struggle with the scoundrel
we know best,
as Gandhi said —

My goal is to live, and live well —
it is the gentle archers' light into the
dark corners of the heart,
speed, power, quickness, all —

21

that makes my goal
a real, lithe thing in the quiver —
beyond time,
beyond borders,
into the green wood of timelessness —
the new real of the chase
for a sundown with the russet sky of Eden.

Sonata for a New Jerusalem

I. Weaving Whole Fabric

Mending the borders,
stitches at a time,
whole fabric,
yards upon yard
of new raiment,
woven of crimson —

I am looking at the life of nations
as the garment of men and women and
break the centuries' lock
on treasured robes,
royal and grand,
fit for real living —

beyond the grip of
mortal sighs and fury,
into the scope and wonder
of clear paces
across the sky.

II. 'Abdu'l-Bahá*

A miracle of timelessness,
this star
I see in the blue of the New Jerusalem,
further than the borders of nations,
He is
the rising of a new dawn,
the true morning star,
high in the resonant rest of His burning pitch.
A diamond blue, azure health,
this point at due East,
within the meanings of the clear rivers of the
mind,
beyond the breaths of dying day,
into the fresh spring
of hyacinths.

III. A Martyr's Blood Is The Stain Of God

Man as man,
woman as woman,
are the fundamentals I seek
in the maverick mind
of one day.

It is
the clouded sea

---

* 'Abdu'l-Bahá (1844–1922) was the Son of Bahá'u'lláh, Founder of the Bahá'í Faith.
He was the authorized Interpreter of its teachings, the perfect example of Bahá'í ideals. He is
well-known for His dedication to promoting Bahá'u'lláh's teachings of brotherhood, the
oneness of religions, the equality of men and women and the elimination of prejudice. The
world's six million Bahá'ís live in over 350 countries, islands and territories throughout
the globe.

to Elysium
that works in me
to say that

time is a rose
and a martyr's blood
is the stain of God —

thus do seasons begin and end
and the Universal Self
I speak of
finds form and flesh.

IV. A Messenger of Glory

A messenger of glory,
the eagle
breathes triumphant life
into a mountain
in his amber flight.

A perfect man,
an absolute woman,
would know the ways
of eagles,

and keep the flight
of this one of nature's angels

in the breast and mind
where nobility could rise
in glances,

and the work of a titan
could appear as rest.

V. Making Day

I am making day
out of the clay and water left
where the potter died.

Some instructions, a wheel,
remain;
it is working the clay,
the climb to the true North
of being,
lucid and redolent,
filled with the fragrance of roses,
trailing into the studio
from his burial place,
everything and nothing in his grasp
over fundamentals,
teaching the gray stones
crimson.

II

From

Living the Boundaries

"Faith is ultimate concern."
Paul Tillich

The Road

Back in the Shenandoah Valley, with work
like the threshing floor in a thorough farm,
to clarify in the concrete, to work on poems . . .
I remember a temperate wind
on Rt. 70,
windows in my Chevrolet wide open,
a steady sense of sailing right through Indianapolis
to Colorado,
there in the rising portals
of a half-spent moon,
that inland place.
A mid-dial rock'n'roll station
the Beatles/Steeley Dan/Paul Simon/
endless mercury vapor lamps coming up, endless.
One by one, along the span of farms, end to end,
like the bales of hay I had worked on the farm,
100 pounds over the shoulder and into the truck.
I closed my eyes and leaned my head back/running
like the freshness of the wind.
Put in a few dollars/a cup of coffee/driving one handed/
the road bent around my mind like the manuscript
envelope/the book I have become.

A constant tension envelope/song by song/
the big sky, large enough to keep
and give away out the side windows.
A round heart now, dark, maybe red enough
to close around the heart of rock'n'roll,
ten miles from Denver/winning the dark side
of the road, riding a messenger of joy/
thumping the wheel over the liberation of my rhyme,

the iconoclasm of it/exile and return/
an odyssey of passion.

On Thoreau

One year is like a thousand
in its sway over seasons.
The formidable grasp of one man
over the details of string, rope,
seeds enough to survive, all
ride into you like the current
of a river sweeping the range
of its own channel.

The new age has a minor prophet,
six thousand miles from Israel.
A fourth generation,
and a fifth must deal with a
man who despised work, kept himself
to odd jobs, and was more than a
nature boy, a sentence-maker
with demands on all of us
to see to the details
of where your conscience lies
when the country has run amuck.

He may be the first man to consult
when making a new start

On Your Own Terms

For Gerald Stern

Of all the nails I ever drove,
the six-inch nail they call a "spike",
the one I left in pine sub-floor over and over,
would be the one I think of as honest.
The spike is true and strong enough
to put a joist in place,
a beam that girds up the house between floors.
Joist to joist, a spike will secure
the joining corners with a lover's drive and grasp.
The stretch of a house across its width and depth
owes itself to a good hammer and a spike.
Steel girders don't do it all.

There is a kind of day when the sun
is relentless, but straightforward enough
so you're glad to have something that works.
Those days, when talk about politics is soaking
through you against your will, the fundamentalists
are pushing you to throw it all to an answer,
and you think you might like to lie down for
fifty years, then decide — then, an afternoon
pounding spikes for the sake of a friend's house
can speak on its own terms.

Good Days

Good days on the road, you had ten dollars
and a tank of gas to start out with,
trying to make five hundred miles.

In a compact, you could fill it one more time,
or put in two or three dollars at a time
along the way. You hoped to keep your thirst
down, and eat one good meal a day.
As often as not, that would be biscuits and gravy
at a truck stop or diner
for under two dollars. The farms
went by like distant relatives,
and you knew you could stop to work
for your meal, a bed, and a few extra bucks.

Still, you went on to the farm you knew best.
Along the Pennsylvania Turnpike,
the lights bore down as if you were
guilty of thinking about a pleasant trip.
It came down to an endurance test
between you and something unworldly,
like your own ghosts of where you hadn't been,
or Jews crossing the desert over
the map of your childhood.

Lexicography Of A Cafe

A cafe is a purple place, sufficient
reason to breathe another breath,

a kind of reason for being,
like the road, or a mountain retreat

you can find in the city.
often enough, there are originals

32

on the walls — a French roast,
or cappucino by the hour — tables outside —

and you can lose yourself
the way saints do in meditation

by going there late at night.
You can peer out at the street and wave

as your friends walk by within reach almost;
you can climb Jacob's ladder

in your reading as they come for a re-fill, or
you can disappear upstairs

into the Zen temple at Kyoto
as you sip some herbal tea —

it is almost illegal to go there
so you can take a look at the night sky

and see where Orion is before you go.
If you work a day job,

and paint evenings and weekends,
it is already known to you, perhaps

in the canvas you picked up in the street
from an old tent. Or maybe

the beauty of God's laughter
has led you there by the song

you have re-found
from twenty years ago,

this cafe, this place for eating destiny,
this overture to the moon.

Fitzgerald Men

My brother and I sat down to dinner
at the Chinese place with nods to each other
as if we were there on business, barely met
an hour before. Gradually, boyish smiles
crept into our eyes and swept our mouths
as we realized the massive privilege,
the immense freedom that was ours —
an entire Friday evening, just us, just the men.
We spent a full twenty minutes, I think,
rehearsing szechuan names and cantonese,
like kung pao beef and moo goo gai pan.
We ordered drinks for our wait,
then something happened in the dream
and we were walking through the city
after our meal, writing our own script
of an Irish folk singer and his friend.
John did get up on the stage to sing,
and I did talk to the girl
the whole time. "Resin the Bow", "The Old
Reuben James", "Isn't It Grand Boys",
then midnight, then 1 A.M. The streets
became a reflection of our steps and
we merged with history, nodded
to each other again, and walked
across the night sky.

Argument For The Existence Of God

A saxophone
/is/sign, miracle, and evidence
enough/for me/
to embrace the idea of God.

Sailing By The Crescent Moon

The crescent moon
is in my memory
like noon,

time enough to stay
where boddhisattvas
wander in and out

like the wind across
the deck of a schooner.

The face of each person
is a sign from God
like the articulate words
from the Buddha Himself.

Having heard them, thus,
having seen the ship of His likeness,
the dockside of His presence
is my first landing.

I am seeing
the breaths of my days

as those purple things
he might have done,
like a trip down the Mississippi, rivers and seas.

Jerry's Sax

A tenor sax in Jerry's hand stirred
the leaves in our town like
the May breeze. He could ride the downbeat
at the edge of a tune straight through
to the end, like his own freight train
across the Plains. His mellow improvisation
put the band in a mood, and things
happened in his hands on that sax
that should not happen. The audience
invariably swayed when he played,
the drummer was a better drummer when he played,
the trumpets declaimed like kings.
The earth disappeared when he got up
into his notes, and the young sound we had
back in 1969 brooded way down until the lava
in us kicked up and shot to the jet stream.

Jerry had control that set you free
and walked across thruways sideways
without making you feel a single bump.
He made wars fade away and stood there
at six foot three inches and found ways to be humble.
When he stood up for a solo, nobody
in the band flinched, and the audience
leaned back for line, speed, and tone
like driving a Mercedes on the Autobahn.

Everything you wanted to happen, happened
with his rides, as we call them,
and when he sat down after sixteen bars,
the band rode out of town without looking back.

Testament

My life is to say "Yes!"
to the inner territory
and the outer journey.
It is to discover a place
to let go of the rage,
a place to simply let go —
it is
to recover from
the death of my angels;
it is to die well,
to live well, inside out.

A Leisure

Time enough to think
remains an imperiled thing,
like a piece of pure coastline,
or a night with only music.

I take myself aside
in the afternoon and nap;
and at the close of day
I weep my fill of consolation
in the arms of Almighty God.

Those Hands, That Face

I watched Artur Rubinstein play
at Constitution Hall, my senior year
in high school, when the master was over 90.
The face was the face of an angel;
the hands were glissandi in themselves.
My accompanist and I froze in attention
as we lost our fears in the immersion
in such quality, such excellence.
Breathless, we dared to take stage seats,
within a glance and a nod of his vision.
Two hands, hummingbirds leaping over one another,
wrapped up in the motion of their harmony,
lived like kings at the end of those arms.
The Steinway gave him a region fitting
that kingship, and the reach and range of the man,
like a prince as might become him, lordly,
swept decibels away from seeing, and lofty men
knelt to see the ivory sweep and lift.

A Resumé

There is a stone in the river
from my first thirty odd years of life.
A book of poems comes this year
at a nice, small press in Maine.
There are references there to work
at the World Bank and to my Quaker College.
But there might be glances
at the Analects of Confucius, the Tao-Te-Ching,
and the idea that the kingdom is a poem.

In any case, lately, I have merged
my vision into a moveable feast
where the coffee (Tanzanian maybe —)
powers the day and I reach
"the mystic through the manic"
along with Roethke, the Northwest poet —
riding "the straws through the fire".

Fixing It Yourself

My father worked as a labor mediator
in Texas during the forties. It was election time

and the Sheriff and his deputies
had commandeered the voting box

to make sure the union didn't win and
certainly, to make sure none of those so-called

undesirables, blacks and hispanics, could vote.
Unarmed, only one hundred and forty pounds,

but 6'1" and duty in his blood
from night flights in World War II,

the Irishman heard about this at his office,
and walked into the place.

He gave the Sheriff and his men
three options — dealing with a Federal law suit,

the hospital or both —
an hispanic man who had been told to leave

turned around and came back to vote
as the Sheriff and his boys got up to go.

Today at sixty-seven and retired, a minister/social worker,
a word from my old man will still cost you your excuses,

and I know middle-aged men
who go to him, as I do,

when they want a straight story,
the prospects for their own bloody histories,

a skeleton key to the Father's House,
a cosmic mechanic you can trust.

Selma, Montgomery and the Army

The orchards over the hills from my parents' house
were full with apples and peaches when my father and I

climbed over the hill to get there, my first time home
from college. He looked up at the sky

as if trying to read the clouds or tell by the moon,
which had come up above the horizon to thirty-five degrees
   or so.

I remember him saying he was happy
after leaving the parish ministry and going into social work –

I could still feel the red breaths
of a Bronx streetfighter as we walked

through the foot-deep hay — his broken nose from the war
and the jeans I wore came under the sway of the moon,

and we decided to turn toward the fallow fields
next to the orchard. As we stood there, finally,

on the top of those Blue Ridge foothills,
he told me about desegregating the mess in the army.

Him, a mere sergeant, seeing black soldiers
forced to sit outside in the mud to eat their C-rations —

storming inside with his .45 unflapped
to tell Major Weimer that he had better

VSget those American soldiers out there
a decent place to eat — inside —

side by side with the rest, or
he would have an angry sergeant to deal with —

as the Major went outside to invite the soldiers in to eat,
my father joined a table of Texans to make sure of his back.

I drove back to Connecticut that night
like the reflection of a star, hoping for northern lights on
the way.

Living the Boundaries

For Paul Tillich

Living the boundaries,
the limbs of an oak

shake the upper boughs
as if to free themselves
of birds, of nests, of leaves —
all things sensible.

The limits beyond limits
are what I have found
in the debate over the real —
like seeing the shell —
perfect and beautiful —
and then the pearl.

The foundations where magma swirls
are my goal, beyond lessons,
beyond prayer, into the agape,
the tao of pure perception,
 where earth and sky meet,
and then disappear.

III

From

New World Suite

"We have a choice to be world citizens or world warriors."

Norman Cousins

Unity-Dancing

I

As the commonwealth of man
rises on the auroral horizon,
we go to the China
we have to come to know and
speak tenderly, forcibly, embraces
to the Soviet-Self
we have left behind —
a friend in the Gulag,
unsung, unbidden to our table.

I go then, to my cafe,
to sing this circle of the sky,
shadow and light,
light upon light,
working out the roses of the Talmud,
the perfume of Allah, Yahweh, Brahma,
and the cafe I linger in is its own universe
in the mind.

II

The claim to vision,
into the peace beyond
this account of war
we read in the news,
leans into the outline
of a century of the Hague,
the League of Nations,
the United Nations,
a Parliament of Man.

There comes an energy
akin to beauty as the decline of beauty
runs head-long into ashes:
kindred wondering about the end of time, then
the phoenix,
off in a certain distance,
like the rising Sun,
Vishnu sends a God-man, oneness Prophet,
Bahá'u'lláh, in a thrush of beauty,
"Peace! Peace!" and
a thousand thousand roses,
nightingales in spring, in spring.

III

Bahá, Exile, Prisoner, Rose,
Timelss Architect,
Tenth Avatar,
Reincarnation of Krishna,
Second Advent,
Prince of Peace, again,
the Mysterious in History,
Buddha of Universal Fellowship,
unity-dancing is the way I have come to know Him.

IV

We re-create time
out of the fabric of timelessness;
He, she, I, we,
weave a garment of crimson
for the Prisoner.

Chains and torture,
forty years,
Isaiah circling around Him, Moses,
Muhammad,
His Odes in rivers
over the plain of Sharon.

V

The Prisoner
For Bahá'u'lláh, the Messenger of God

1

Prisoner, Exile,
Rose, Scion of Law,
Miracle of Reason —

2

Crimson Justice,
Eden's Phoenix, Man's Question,
Heaven's Answer —

VI

For our new vision, our regeneration,
with earth at spring,
its silo of winter ready,
I wake,
teeming prayers in my days,
like the ear of ritual,
devotion's incense,
bhakti, love,

I read the Bhagavad-Gita
of the Hindus
past midnight,
and rise at dawn.

VII

My joy days
spent in the bosom of
the Song of Songs,
the Beatitudes,
the Epistles,
Isaiah's roundness, His garden,
His temple of grandeur,
charging us to wideness.

The pearl.
The Crimson Ark of Bahá/escort in time/
out of time/
            seasons in Jerusalem, New Jerusalem,
         Ganges valley, Yangtse shadows, Nairobi nights,
            Delhi days, Dharma days, Kyoto,
         shadow and light, refraction of time,
                unity-dance.

VIII

Thus, the commonwealth of man,
brotherhood and sisterhood,
this Tree of Life,
we are called
like earth and sky,
into the calamity of its reason,
like the remembrance of the moon,

Alláh'u'Abhá! Alláh'u'Abhá!

Rising Sun/aura of gladness/
   tempest time wrung out of time/
         Alleluia! Alleluia!
    sundance/unity-dance/fling the cord of joy/high! high!

IX

"You can kill me,
but you cannot stop the emancipation of
women!"
cries Ṭáhirih, the feminist poet,
at her execution.

In the stillness of midnight,
the center of the universe is fire and light,
and a rose,
like that light upon light,
so often on the tongue of the son of Bahá'u'lláh,
'Abdu'l-Bahá, so strong, so tender.

X

I am immersed in the sea
of a New Jerusalem,
with those same rivers of Eden,
flowing through my mind.

I know stones by the river
and the tidal sensibility of an ocean.
I am coming to see
the green grass of Sharon
as gold, silver, treasure beyond treasure;

I gather the cypress to my mind
like the incarnation of virtue;

I fly over the hyacinth rainbow
I heal by;

a wonderer, sacred and worldly, like seas,
I search galaxies and become a star/
climb out of the mind into
things in themselves.

XI

The simple, the rich,
the poor, the Brahmin,
the underclass, the scholars,
all heard the new vision with praises.
I am won in the key of G to this wonder,
I am won in E flat,
I am won in F.

I am won in ragas,
lotus is my flower,
New Delhi is my far away, fly away home.
I am won in Be-Bop
as Dizzy Gillespie,
for fifty years,
plays the horn, so beautiful, so full of love,
happy-feet,
unity-dance,
a Bahá'í, this Dizzy.

XII

Roses, roses,
the Ode to Joy of Beethoven

in the time of Bahá,
declaring the oneness of the human race,
Dostoevsky, the same universal,
all on a Pegasus wind.

I carry my words
home to the farm,
home to the city,
far into and out of the mind of the maker,
across the careening sky.

XIII

I have wound my words around this Tree
and climb it like ivy;
I "redeem the time"
and remember, upon waking,
Rimbaud.
Roses are my chief concern,
art and religion embracing like fire and air,
a thousand years of peace,
time.

XIV

"The earth
is but one country
and mankind its citizens"
declares the Prophet.
The closing of these borders
whirls us
into the Global Village, a Union of States,
beyond blood-letting,
into a new meaning,
thrust by history's own fire.

Coming, coming,
Oslo, Prague, Beijing,
Moscow, New York,
Jerusalem,
new world, rising.

XV

We wring entropy out of time,
timelessness in time,
a centripetal force,
like the weaver's threads upon a spool,
a choreographed thing,
so divine, so awful,
"such courage, such passion",
I remember Rilke saying we must
"hold to the difficult".

XVI

I am Jew,
I am Christian,
I am Moslem,
I am Buddhist,
I am Hindu,
I am Bahá'í,
then, in its oneness,
its unity-dance,
like the wings of the dove in motion,
I pray for peace,
and sweetly smell roses,
woodsmoke and honey in my own Shenandoah Valley,

hyacinths and anemones, acrosss my years,
dying daily toward a good death,
the clay broken,
phoenix-rising.

XVII

The andante clarinet
on the recording in my room,
here, as I write,
remembering
the concert of Rubinstein
in the year of my graduation,
on stage,
within view of his previous
hands,
my accompanist and I,
breathless.

XVIII

The rainbow lingers;
we are ready, steadily working,
rising to a world
commonwealth,
our gaze steady on peace.

Language
redeems culture, it must;
and southern writers
renew us.

As Bahá'ís, then,
we are like reeds

out of a marsh, me,
a sprig of timothy,
bending to hear and breathe
the peace dream.

XIX

One day I went walking
in the tangled web of
lightning, rain and darkness
to hear Joyce:

the Dead, the Dead, the Dead,
pitched in the motion of that seeing,
brewing, yeasting,
a time out of time,
suffering, making and remaking myself/
epiphanies following.

Living the Color Crimson

I

Jerusalem embraces America in my mind,
on the fifth year after a trip to Israel;

I see Arabs and Jews, Moslem, Christian, all
as the stars of one velvet sky,

heaven shared with Buddhist, Hindu and Confucian, equals;
the work of living peace, one vision,

Quetzalcoatl, side by side with Moses and Muhammad,
living religion as the Tao of all religions;

humanity is my religion, living moral excellence my goal,
roses my day and night, the glory of sacrifice, my wings.

II

I like to think of being Bahá'í as
living as well as a gazelle runs,
being human in the image of eagles;

if dolphins are precious and beautiful,
so may be Bahá'ís, whether they bear the name
or not; I am thinking of ideal beings, like stars.

Something has fallen apart at the center of time
in our century; looking for an answer
has come to be as common as crisis;

I think of Bahá'í as the Easter
of a century of blood, as
the oneness of all humans, the epiphanies

of going to bed to the moon, and
waking to birdsong, as all-excelling as
being human well, as generous and bold
as the ocean itself.

III

Just over the hill
in my Shenandoah Valley town,
there are old orchards

where once I walked with my father.
In the mid-season
tumult of burgeoning apple trees,
we heard the bowing branches creak
with their fruitage.
That walk,
possibly taken more than once,
if memory serves,
is my pilgrimage to Israel;

it is the peace
and the red breaths of history, mind in time,
my/our,
like New York, my father/World War II night flights/
like the Western Wall,
the Mount of Olives,
Mount Carmel,
peace, eternity, roses.

IV

To the witness of Eden,
there is little here in the way of blizzards,
but storm is
the reminder of the cruelty of history,
the hard lines of a well-planned battle, here, now,

as 140 nations gather in New York
to make plans for peace. No answers,

no way out,
only phoenix-fire burning.

V

The rest of doing
carries me,
like the piano man
who only wants to play his piano.

I live to be
and these poems are
my existence,

my heady aura
against the dark.

VI

I was
the only white man
in a gospel choir,
and the only white man
in a black jazz band.

My trumpet
still knows its way
to a sweet tone and
plays me to sleep
with a listening ear
to midnight.

I meditate with it, too,
and know myself better
because of its healing.
I choose a deli
where women, professionals,

students, working class,
black and white
come freely
to the music
of Gershwin's magic:
jazz, classical,
and these Dylan tapes, others.

I remember Freddie Hubbard's first trumpet
was made
of a funnel and a garden hose
and keep to an old portable.

The shirt I wear today has the scripts
of six languages:
English, Russian, Hebrew, Japanese,
Greek and Arabic.
There is this race we must run.

Fritjof Kapra writes the *Tao of Physics*,
and my mind is bent
towards the fusion of two lovers,
science and religion,
embracing in the thoughts
of a physicist
outside the temples of Kyoto.

VII

Hope and despair intertwined
are the roses I live.
I learn of things as they are
by leaving them.

I see the host
and linger over it, sniff
the communion wine,
and move on.

Still,
I ache for liturgy,
for ritual,
for patterns
large enough to be a net
under days, days enough, full enough
to ride me high
into dying day.

VIII

On an odd day
I go to Quaker meeting or
discuss the Unitarian-Universalist Church
with my friend Paul.
There is so much of me that is wide and empty,
gaping,
agnostic like night.
Bahá'u'lláh speaks of God as the "Unknowable Essence".

I find this indefinite universe,
wide as time,
my own days as leonine as a century, at least
these thirty-odd years;
my meandering
as mortal as roses,
as incomplete as a single cherry table
without its room.
Feeling this wideness,

like the sea,
this bliss and ease of my untended garden,
I wind out my themes in song,
the blustering Irishman who is my father,
my mother, the composer of twenty children's musicals,
my brother, my sister, competent and kind,
these poems in the Shenandoah Valley like rain.

IX

I rehearse the tide of giving.

I look for this victory of peace,
against the background of the disappearing dead:
dachau/watts/tet/Dr. King/Kennedy/Kennedy,

then charge myself
like a wave turning in upon itself
with the work here.

I will hide in the rock
and find my solace
in the ports of 140 nations.

X

On my knees;
university for the temple begins here.
Say your graces, and
do the fast at Yom Kippur,
for they are listening at the rabbi's table.

Still,
I remember
the single cherry blossom.

XI

I am as good as any amorous man
and cry over my Lord
with hard tears.

I seek only the resonant stone
in the light of light itself,

tying,
weaving,

the broken strands,

In my afternoon,
a global studies major,
working on his poems,

in my evening
a Bahá'í Chinese,
who remembers

his traditional family there,
blending Taoist, Confucian, Buddhist,
as the very epitome
of Chinese religion.
The next day,
coming into conversation
over pastries and coffee
with a Bahá'í who teaches at the Quaker school nearby.

It is a coming into conversation.

Now
at the Hamburg Inn,
a resolute heart,
next to the athlete,
remembering two years
driving a cab
for the senior citizens.
Nods to the retired farmer
at the table —
conversation opens up
into this complete embrace,
roses,
the fragrance of anemones,
living the color crimson.

IV

From

God's Whimsy

"Laughter is spiritual relaxation."
'Abdu'l-Bahá

The Holy Passions

For William Butler Yeats

Give me the holy passions —
the high ambitions of the Rose —
for Ireland loves a martyr
and wide is the needle's eye in mercy —

Everything says either yes or no
to Eden, to Gilead, to Jerusalem,
and this is the wide embrace —

I am concerned with the music,
the music of epiphanies all year long,
and Easters in the heart of the average person —

it is hot cries in the desert,
followed by sweet, pouring water,
wrought out of God's own giving —
a giving so complete, so total,
that it is won
just by going,
just by believing that much
in the endless pageant of human need.

Reflection

In the latitudes the heart lives,
I see the relentless discovery
of the touchstones that remake us —

Through the brutal breakers
thrown at us, the human spirit,
regal, defiant, triumphant, reeling,

solves itself in some indeterminant code,
some lucid gamble on its own sovereign odds,
a high braille that can only be called mystery —

Lions of God

December 10, Human Rights Day, 1989

Freedom is a bell,
a meaning, a quiet sacred sounding
here, now, as the lions free themselves —
reluctant lions maybe,
but urgent like poems,
these bulletins from the belly of the world —
Walesa — Gorbachev — the Chinese students —
surging with the days like waves —
angled as tangents to the unreal —
here, then, the first black governor —
a new world coming, Blue —
me, I am thinking of the lions,
witting, unwitting, named, unnamed,
the lions of God, roaring like sun-stars —

Blue Reason

I am thinking of a blue reason
that drives the old badlands down,
a core bliss coming like a new moon,

I mean, an ancient new real
holding up the new Eden, oh Father God, oh, oh,
my sweet Mother God, remember me,
my spent days, spending all the coin on this,
one separate joy after another,
God-songs to draw on,
humming rides from Dizzy,
old lover-dove Holy Spirit,
nailing down the is —

An Ardor for Peace

An ardor for peace
wears well,

like an old tartan,
a knit scarf around the neck —

it is a health of its own —
a sky blue health —

I sing its joy-springs —
a distilled water lifted with laughter —

it is a tough-tender ride
at the cosmic carnival —

it is that luck of the devoted
that rides us into the New Jerusalem by sundown —

67

Breakfast

In the hotel in Jerusalem
we ate whole raw fish,
whole loaves of bread,
whole eggs, hard-boiled,
and black olives, five or six different kinds —
each dish served in a basket,
twenty of them or so,
around the table, including
several kinds of bagels,
a separate bucket each
for jellies, butter and cream cheese —
I thought I would never finish
when an armed guard
flooded through the hotel lobby
out past a French import —
the morning had exploded
and the soldiers would hitchhike
from there to the front line in Lebanon —
bending the meaning of justice
to a marching tune we never heard —

Numinous — Word, Lake and Power

Numinous, that word, speaks it —
no, the theologians have used it up —
yet, it meant light, luminous wondrous light —
the hard variety, that rigorous light —

I am thinking of the calloused hands
someone gets from handling a rare book collection —

the speaking it is to see a coal miner face on –
I am thinking of the man who goes to the diner, once,
does not stay as I have, that man, riding
a fine car, wonderful home, but heart enough to care
seeing that the working class needs a caring eye –
a hard diamond mind of compassion –
a regal levity at the right moment in negotiations –
a close reading of a talmudic tradition –
soundless feet at a Buddhist temple –
some real knowledge of Japanese tea ceremony –

I am thinking of priceless pearls passed by,
the merest wind of truth searched out,
hundreds of miles to swim in an honest lake –
this is a hint of what the theologians mean –

Jazz Song

Sitting in the cafe,
listening to the blues,
reminds me of the Blue Wisp Jazz Club
in Cincinnati, taking in the club trio,
a piano man, bass and drums,
like the Ohio River running
through your mind, rush, surge and whip,
no need to go to New York to hear them,
just sit there in the waves of sound –
later in the set, a sax man joins them,
lets the club rip wide open –
a bass player comes to mind,
one who says, "Yeah, man, I blow bass,"

as if his fingers were wind —
so I drive my feet to town after this,
best car I ever had,
tickling myself to hear Cincinnati Joe Duskin
fly off the poster at the Blue Wisp,
and drop onto the Vineyard,
riding his piano.

The Last Riverboat

I hopped a ride on the last riverboat,
the Delta Queen, and rode from Cincinnati
to Louisville — a sax man, a mezzo-soprano
and I danced our way from the School of Music
at Indiana to the port, laughing our way
to the darkness, where the river passed
beneath us, around us, almost through us,
with a black sheen that absorbed light
the way a torch engulfs the dark —
I worked half the trip,
tossing down my linen napkin,
folding chairs, folding up tables,
helping the old black men,
getting a five dollar tip —
in Louisville, we spun the paddlewheel
almost by ourselves into dockside —
the singer at the best jazz club in town
joined us — four sets and five rounds
later, we chased down the blues
at an old dive across town
where she wrapped herself around the microphone
and sang "Kansas City" and the rest of the blues til dawn.

In Sum

Below the ledge of earth,
there, in the holocaust room,
as death's starlings cackle,
I am confident of this, still —

that from our groaning bones,
hung with flesh or not,
comes a dark light
that builds the city on the hill —

God's Whimsy

God's whimsy
    is to create Himself
thousands of millions of different ways,
    universes, making Himself,
        God's whimsy is to create man who creates —

I don't think God is past tear-jerkers,
        for what is it to send a young man
    into the lions —
        all at stake, life, principle, property,

God's eye is on the Roman in the crowd
        who cannot give up position, but
        breathes to himself that this is wrong —

God's whimsy could be
    the Blue Angel pilots and their jets,

a peaceful, peacetime sort of mission,
to fly endless flight in close formation,
    to twirl and twirl and twirl,
screaming by over crowds,
    neglecting their own safety,
    emancipating the human need to
        soar —

God's whimsy
likens itself to a cool-warm day in July
    sitting on enclosed balconies, overlooking
a Martha's Vineyard scene,
    glasses of iced tea, tipped with lemon,
yearning for nothing at all,
    content with the absolute glory of no,
        delighted with yes,
    overcome with the grandeur of not quite,
        maybe dear, let's not today —

God's whimsy
must be like the canopied beds
    meant for wealthy couples,

for one night given to a poor lad
        and his girl,

        wonderful couple sort of things happening,
        a joyful noise is made,

morning breaks over our little vacation,
        God smiles

God's whimsy
   is among the soldiers who
      at a truce,
come up to the demarcation line to chat —

   God's whimsy is there
      in the diner
   where the food is so cheap
   you can eat there every day,
and so good you want to —

   God's whimsy
   resides with the Persian sage
      who tells humorous stories
among America's wealthy and sophisticated,
      leaving religion aside —

God's whimsy is
   like the shade trees you always wanted,
and maybe had, trees under which nothing
      happened, over and over again.
   in such totally wonderful ways
      that no one could quite recall
until years later, just how glorious it was

      O I am so tired
being productive, caring about the news,
   I think I will stop wearing socks,
I will forget to buy new shoes,
   I will leave my shoe laces untied a few days,
then, I will eat my fill of food and sleep awhile,
      and remember that I am not so handsome anymore,

73

and I have no real money of my own,
  but God's whimsy may be wishing me to live,
  God's whimsy may be in my bones, making days
    come and go —

Logos

I am singing the open question
  of how to speak through
as a horse may ride through a thicket —

the opportune moment, the quiet relatedness,
  I am speaking of making connections,
the quotidian, the quiddity, the tertium quid —

The querulous yearning to break free,
  it is this that drives me,
I am working myself, this tough-tender,

I am impelled toward the divine in this,
  and toward the new real in the world,
the spiritual-humanist new real, up-ending —

O mystery, O logos
  music of the divine,
Christian — Jewish — Buddhist heart —

try in us, your clarity of soul,
  blend in us your visible soothing yes,
let the click in us, click, let being be —

O my friend, 'Abdu'l-Bahá,
　　break forth in new vision,
Show forth your plenitude,

Exact your price of high intent,
　　forswear your price,
Embrace, hug, demur, defer, and we too, yes —

O my friend 'Abdu'l-Bahá,
　　grace, dignity, sureties of our days,
but O your divine jokes,

your plenteous humor, up-ending
　　the self-satisfied answers,
the crucial self-effacement in yours, showing you

Let this bracing brace,
　　let this shower cleanse,
let anger abate, let jealousy mend,

O Scion of Spirit, 'Abdu'l-Bahá,
　　O Son of Bahá,
Embrace us again, for we are weary —

Crescent heart, moon delight,
　　visit us, lest we perish,
O Divine, bring forth our heraldry —

Fix in us, then, the axioms of being,
　　list in our emblem hearts
the new name, the crucial Bahá —

Fix in us the absolute,
    then, blend it with your tenderness,
Show us the path, then, let us walk it,

O Friend, let us dawdle a bit,
    let us be nobodies together,
Let us be somebodies in the next moment —

O reluctant divining questor,
    my great vow,
O joy, O consolation, O confidant,

Ah, me, 'Abdu'l-Bahá, what was it,
    fifty years in prison?
House arrest, exile, O your plenitude —

You know the self so thoroughly,
    O Master, O Christ-like —
Evidence all around you, in you, through you —

It is such difficult bliss to know you,
    such an outlandish heart
in an established sort of character —

O my mentor, my taskmaster,
    "Create in me a pure heart,"
"renew in me a tranquil conscience" —

For you can, my friend, you have mastered it,
    you have made fine art and effectual bliss
Out of the lattice work of spirit —

V

From

Rhapsody

"Whither can a lover go but to the land of his Beloved?"
Bahá'u'lláh

Gentle me, my lamp, my luminous
touch, kindle, win me,
ambient angel —

show me your lean eyes,
ineluctable eyes, redolent eyes,
spin me through your universes

there in your limbs,
send me through your fusion self,
your Source, your beginnings —

2

lay me down on your handsome lay,
your weave of loveliness,
your generous rest —

gentle me down, and I will lift you
like a kite, my banner, my drink,
and I will be your prize —

each of us winding out our loftiness,
like the tuck of a jib,
like a thorough regard for breezes —

3

Blend this roaring heart
with your dark brilliance,
ebony on ivory in our eyes —

a readiness in the bowing stars,
a sharp longing warmed by morning,
you, my lute to play, I, your clavier,

or, do you want a piano, forte and all,
largeness, room, spaces,
keys to spring a bit —

4

Maybe the genius of your singularity
lies in your fierce achievement,
your total loving —

so, we succeed as a work, if we do,
only because you surge with enthusiasm
for my doing, and I for yours,

winning the portals of the mind,
reading the old world as it passes away,
imagining new worlds to live —

5

New, old, locked on, waking to see,
just to see, exactly what shape it is
to overcome ourselves, our foolish selves,

the rudiments of change, these flawed selves,
harrowed for change, planted,
spun out for new growing –

I begin myself in the wordless spaces
where the mind fixes on itself,
ridding itself of itself –

finding its longing in the flesh,
ridding itself of the flesh,
sporting the flesh,

heading up a project, myself,
riding a whim, myself,
God's whim –

riding my riding, into the road,
falling into the road for itself,
forgetting and remembering, remembering and forgetting –

7

I silence myself
in order to be,
to breathe —

this releases something
larger than I am, and
this otherness

depends on you
to sample its rightness
like blocks of cheese —

8

I wrap my arms
around you like a life
meeting a life —

a day hinged to a day
making a possible core
that calls life into being,

across time, rolling,
praying its way through walls,
making holes in the calendar —

We shape our listening
out of the original letters
of our common alphabet

that only we know,
these trips, these meals aside,
our late nights,

listening to it all,
it breathes a commonness with others, too,
like the limbs of things —

Leaning into my life,
I send my wounds
to my heart, and

my heart kneads them,
tugs at them, signs them,
and delivers them to the lungs of humanity

to breathe as purified air,
as the heuristic bones
that dredge mercy's channel —

The silences become more,
the loam underneath, richer,
all, a kind of gift —

I do, and I sing,
yes, I play trumpet,
I miss appointments,

and like myself besides,
like a favourite braided rug
that has been in the family for years —

I am hitched to a small corner
in Cincinnati, a boat on the Vineyard,
a small piece of history,

so I walk away from myself,
into emblems of gratitude,
emblems of congratulation,

the members of my family, vehement service,
vehement humility, intense pride,
fierce loyalty, all in my family, in me —

I want to feel directly,
there, in your precious arms,
resonant with being, like trees,

the trees, healing us,
as the reach of our lives turns back
into our too obvious mortality,

naming us, meeting us, there,
in a beach, a drive, a new friend,
Selma, Washington, past illusion —

We rise into the definite wings
we know as the huge lightness
of the love itself,

I look at your ample eyes,
and very possibly begin to fuse
with you across the table —

I sometimes think we throw
occasional no hitters, the two of us,
there in the cafe, no errors either —

A license to joy is what we take,
or maybe we take nothing at all,
surrounded by everything as it is —

it is a seacoast self we live,
a mountain self, a street bazaar
that pins us to the new real —

slicing away at the self,
still, a conundrum and an oddity,
the ego as identity and inflammation —

16

Nonetheless, I see, feeling beyond
the tractable mind, like the circus musician
who shows real heart, playing down-line,

playing anyway, the jazz musician's
moon and shadow, putting it out there,
no razor blade mind, but dreams —

so I sit there in the kitchen and
listen to the morse code of these moments,
tangible lists of urgency —

VI

From

Planet Dreams

"We are the consciousness of the earth."
Joseph Campbell

Planet Dreams

I am dreaming an urge,
there, in the forcible core of the planet,
there, in the primal dark,
primal light itself,
cutting crystalline windows,
forming mosaic tile, yet
how much more, forging the new order,
out of the genius of our hearts,
this new thing, this new ardor,
breaking the waves over our impossible heads,
phasing new bridges to ourselves,
this present as the history of the future,
the future as a new music,
planet dreams to dream,
the singing of a new song,
rising out of the vortex,
into a phoenix song
where earth spins by the very force of love,
giving our ruined hearts
an ache to live —

Floating on the Edge

I sat there at the edge,
the edge where you lean over
and look at the roots of the world
from sixty-thousand feet —
and I locked onto the idea that
God could be found by floating —
I proved this out

over a span of forty-five hundred test flights —
which just goes to show
that a good hypothesis
can overcome a shortage
in laboratory equipment
and university budget —
despite the odds that
experimenters can explode
on atmospheric re-entry
wearing only blue jeans and a flannel shirt —

Shadow and Stone

I leaned into the shadows
the mind cast off —
losing whole histories of myself —
but found a larger God than before,
one who could break my fears
like dead branches and
use them for fuel —
there in the darkest place of all,
the shattered soul,
I discovered the quirky God
who could laugh with me,
realize a dream larger than my hopes,
and put it all away
in the hip pocket,
like a stone,
to polish and dream on again —

Blues After Midnight

I sit here deluged by debt,
burgeoning luck has collapsed,
brain drain has hit my own —
the ideas have split for the West Coast —

I make guesses about sleepwalking
through the rest of the century,
living the next breath by faith alone,

no saving graces in sight,
no resurrections by morning,
just the blues to drive me down
after midnight —

The Soul qua Soul

The soul dives into itself
then, is surrounded by soul —
it is letter and envelope —
its own question and its own answer —

the soul qua soul is
terrain, geography, home —
the soul is map of being —
a country to itself —

Earth Song

I am looking at green, green life
going back towards time like rivers,

or ground water in its own cavernous law,
toward the reinvention of Eden.

It is a thousand roses,
An Avatar, the realization of the real,
like the first Tree.

The joy of its ready steam
to ride clover to the ocean

is the side of the day
opened like a compass

to the re-alignment of earth,
like a new ship on one ocean —

Atlantic, Pacific, Indian,
Mediterranean, Adriatic, Arctic —

I see the source in the source of wind,
and the meaning of memory is the river Tigris,

the river Ganges, the Yangtse, my Amazon hopes,
the tug of the Mississippi toward Orion.

Transportation

I sit here, 6 A.M.,
on a Saturday, riding
through the grey mist,
still riding foolish,
in the counter seat at the diner —
driving the car to Maine,

riding the train to New York, to Boston —
riding in the plane to Israel
where soldiers are still
hitchhiking in civilian Volvos
to the front of Lebanon — with M-16s —
I am still in school, listening
to a lecture, here in the chair —
I am riding the lesson back home
from college to research migrant labor
and I am driving to Washington
to work for a Nader group —
I am on the subway to work —
I am reading the morning *Post* in my chair
and I am rocking in your arms —

Portrait

For my brother

John leaps up the stairs
three at a time,
up from the street door
of Defenders of Wildlife,
the Washington office.
At the top of the steps,
the door to his office is to dance with,
and the phone is for instant replays
of the office tailback,
hanging up, then, soaring
across the room to kick the door shut,
like Karate Kid. Law is made for Don Quixote.
White knights and Irishmen
gather at a nearby pub

to hold a wake for corporate polluters.
And play is the buckler and
chief research tool of the attorney.

Wake the Dead

Wake the dead, brother,
make a list, do something,
act straight, act hip,
be foolish, cock-eyed,
re-write the Book of the Dead, sister,
read the Analects of Confucius,
read the thing upside down,
invoke the saints, Dimaggio,
Mantle and Mays,
go home, leave home,
rock in your lover's arms,
just to spite the church,
aim — aim — and fire!
no guns! no war!
fight for your beliefs!
fight for your flag!
fight for old GM! no fighting!
be proud! be humble!
find the root of Ireland,
learn Gaelic, and
be sure to swim the Atlantic —

Going To The Universe

"I'll be going
to the universe today, dear,

don't wait up.
Naturally, I'll call
when I find a hotel,
Be sure to water the plants
and don't forget
to change the sun.
I may be gone for awhile,
Do give my best
to geology,
and remember me to physics —
it's been so long.
I miss you already,
my dear, dear planet, so long —
your moon loves you —
bye-bye . . ."

The Struggle for Meaning

The struggle for meaning is a tree —
it is a river singing of itself —
this journey sense is a meaning becoming itself —

hours are meanings —
days are centuries —
years change whole societies —

each poem releases energies —
each thought is a sacred gift from out there —
each hazardous duty done is a martyrdom —
each solid day of work is the worth of a deacon —

Journal Poem

I sit here, typing, making myself,
readying myself to die,
death, as the quiet empty spaces that
churn you up and toss you back to life —
rummaging around in the mind,
as if it were an attic —
waiting for the right moment,
the moment when I exist, when
life finds me, and I am somehow this special thing —
waiting, for waiting, for life, waiting
to see what gorgeous thing I think next for me.
somehow pointing to myself, somehow not,
putting on my shoes, stroking, tying, stroking,
up the stairs from the studio, out,
puttering away into town for morning coffee, diner,
what lovely people who do not speak of books —
these, my townsmen, who know the weather and
how to go hunting without shooting anything —

Classic Case

Classic case — there I am,
sitting like some kind of innocent,
waiting for my pizza,
then the spiritual boom falls —
two guys in black leather jackets
toss open the door as if
it were a matchstick —
two blonde girls walk in —
heavy metal song #1

96

blasts the back of my head off —
various epithets fly between
the supposed lovers —
push, shove, and hug —
they place their order,
then, sit down to wait,
staring at me and the walls
as if life were the enemy —
ten minutes — their pizza - "Let's ride" —

Guilt, Fear and Pure Rotten Karma

I am taking the decade
to work the losses off —
not that I have a ledger,
but I can register the deficits,
ticking off the downside,
as if the guilt, fear, and
pure rotten karma
were tangible dross —
no, no murders to account for,
at least so far, no felonies,
just unpaid parking tickets,
half-run red lights, those orange ones,
shameless jealousy of good writing,
last place blues, no matter how I'm doing,
the social register to worry about,
see how I'm doing with the aging hippies,
senseless lack of addiction to worry about,
I mean, what is the point of living if
your only bad habit is diet cokes,
nothing left to count except the vague hint

that somehow, somewhere, I was wrong
to feel the slight rise of the chest,
letting go — middle class, slave-driving self forever.

Colorado Spruce

I wanted to be a willow
I've wanted to be a pine
I love the dear dogwood and
I know a red maple nearby —

But I think today,
I'll be the Colorado Spruce
my father has planted
in the back of our house —
a lofty blue-green —
settling in for fifty years of growth,
by the shade of the mountains,
the crystal accompaniment of
the river's song —

Night, Night Listen Well

Night, night listen
to these troubles, night —
you can hide them
in your disappearing self —
you know a black hole
to steal away to —

all the meter is gone,
all the stanzas reel off
into space, the couplets
sting like overgrown children —
I am an iamb to myself —
neither more nor less,
simply being in time —
mortal, refused, denied, found,
and molded to some hand of unsure destiny —
take these away night,
take these meanings
off the wall and
make them day.

Insomnia

It must be 3 A.M. and
here I am reading the want ads,
listening to the radio,
bed turned down, rumpled,
costing me 12 cents an hour
in lights to keep it highlighted
in this nice little melange
I have going here —

insomnia must be a friend,
a strange, unwanted friend
who comes over to visit after midnight —
not the strangler, just an unwanted sort
who drives you to even more caffeine
just to spite yourself,

something to do with the hands
besides smoke — oddities of a straight man,
insomnia getting all the laughs from
the purveyors of sleeping aids
and late night television —

VII

A Book of Questions

"Live the questions."
Rilke

Can a square melt
into a round?
Can a double-down demon fit
into paradise, sideways?
Can a Christian fit
into a Hindu hum?
Where is a jazzman
if he is not up on the roof swaying?
Can a diplomat whirl?

Buddha Force/Christ Force

Primal force at the center of time,
avatar, phoenix —

Revelation wings, that bird,
consequential voice —

Building in your speech, fire in language,
life urge —

Making the mind of man and woman
into pure soul —

Seeing a unity in the variousness
of beings, all, out of clay —

To see you is to live Moses —
To be in you is to grasp Abraham —

103

In your mirror of history,
things in themselves shine fresh —

out of all beings,
you are a possible river —

Augury

We shall see
what the forcible phoenix
shall do, undo, forgive
and place into service here.
The shape of staccato,
warm and hot fires of love
may be the release
of the bird
from its shadowed cage
beyond the place
where Styx
could sing its dolour.

The New Unthinkable

The new unthinkable
of one planet arrives on a leaf
from Moscow.

The Origin of Singing

The whole heuristic hum
there, in the absolute trees,

lives like a perfect song,
in the resolute heart —

a certain reeling joy
careens off the sky,
creating a way to see
out of the rimmed hearing
where God sings the hours,
we listen to the song,
forming a tradition of singing,
out of the most resonant clay —

Violette in G

I rose to the earth's song
and saw the perfect phoenix
flying the dance of everyone —
and still someone, so pure, so sweet —
I rose to the earth's song
and held the fire, there
in my resolute eyes, and watched
the perfect phoenix,
singing the earth's song.

American Song

I listen to a country song
here in Virginia's Valley,
and I wonder over
the body politic.

We just had the Chinese New Year –
Here, on this side of the river, as elsewhere,
it is Black History Month –
it was just Carnival for Mexico –
Blarney for Erin on March 17th –
England, dear England –

It is the new day dawning –
it is the cost and joy of coming home –

Cloister

The paneled basement has become a shelter
for the pondering of a Quaker College graduate.
In its silence, it is a retreat from the formless
mechanical world. In the hurly burly
shoving match, a geopolitics of neutrons,
I search the temperate words of Dante
for the re-worked planet. Erasmus and More
visit me in their redoubtable leanings,
favor of some unsung angel in the next room.

After Celebration

Since yesterday, my eyes
have ailed for the brown earth,
having seen the brilliant sun.
The things I count worthy, then,
will combine with this terra firma –

A portion of food, a love, music,
patience and courage — something
ods bodkins enough
to keep spring in winter.

The Disciples

Twelve tears fell
from God's eyes
and soothed him
for a while. The lesson
they taught the fool
who was watching
was that stones can sing
and oceans were his own
failed tears — scorching
the cheeks of his own
bleeding majesty.

Judgment Day

The sound of the sea stirred
like ice breaking, like thunder
and superlative lightning in the East.
The sinews of reason snapped
and the chords of hearing ripped open.
The reserve of my culture
broke open into this river.
Many paths veer and converge
at the vortex of a century of
exploding, vertical "Yes" —

"The strife is o'er, the battle won" —
"Peace" cries the Prophet —
and we pursue it in 170 nations
across the world "running to and fro".

Report to the United Nations

This fellow Gorbachev,
this leonine, slip-shape of a dove,
arrives today to
"undo the logic of the nuclear arms race" —
still, the American President
is a tiger with his eyes
softly glowing
in an age of hollow men.
Reagan escorts the angel
of incendiary love
into the white hotel
where presidents and premiers
wrestle with Athens mortality.
They set out to enslave the will to war
and free the world
from the peculiar, the torrid anxiety
of a precipice.

State of the World

In the pure, reliable dark,
I write a crescent moon
of how the world is becoming
awkwardly itself, defiantly
itself — catastrophically itself —

ethnicity is a salvation, yet
with a trigger — most of the
peacemakers are religious,
as well as most of the war-mongers —
the World Bank is very much a bank,
too little for the world —

of all the silences, there are
those that fall between friends —
how the Japanese hear their own
footsteps, and how the Europeans
are aghast at American arrogance —

how we need each other nonetheless —
how the hungry dive down into
their hunger, coming up with strands
of the U.N. — above all, we need
to make sure of our brick and mortar —
to make sure there is something,

something in the chest — to assure
the future we were made of bone and marrow —

The Day of Forgiveness

The ivory of my maker
and the ebony of my maker
roil within me with all races
and the hope of nations

lingers in the refrain of
Lowell, "For Every Man and Nation
Comes the Moment to Decide",
sung in slavery times, undoing.

A Testament of Roses

I saw a rose petal
and wept my tears
for the martyrs
of every race,
of every land,
of every religion,
ever — then I saw
the delicate phoenix
return to earth
and leave.

Denoting Avatar

The word Avatar is a semiotic rose petal
like the rear view of Sunday
in a Christ-Spirit/Hindu window.
I am seeking the "angle of ascent"
with Hayden toward the portrait of time
in the real, luminous sky of the garden.
The color blue is my vision of peace and
the color crimson is my daily immersion
in a sea of sensibility.

A Song for Pops Armstrong

In the out, up the over,
    I am going back to Eden,
well may swinging swing again,
    for Ellington plays there,
yes, Billy Strayhorn writes some tunes,
    and Doc Holladay plays bari,
well, am we going to swing in Eden,
    for Dizzy blow down the walls again —

Jericho, Jericho, go away Jericho,
    Dizzy blow us home to Eden —

A Song of Circles

Joining myself to the circle,
I live a circle —

endlessly rounded music,
tonal and sonorous,

I weep my assonance,
my tears are in this consonance —

how delighted I am to go beneath
the heart of tears to hear

the blue moon humming
her song of circles —

There Are Many Ways of Saying Yes

Here, in the Virginia countryside,
a country song vamps in,
cutting me close to the belly of the South —

"there are many ways of saying yes" —
so a Yale friend once said of Nietsche —

so did Nietsche praise the Buddha and Christ
the paragraph after saying "God is dead" —

so does the vortex deepen and grow velvet —
well may we consider the honesty
a serious nude gives to canvas —

what then, residing in the human heart,
embraces all things at its most God-like —

what olive-skinned cinnamon soul
falls utterly welcome amid ivory —

Tanka

I think God grows,
metamorphoses,
by epochs,
as a human life will in decades —
vibrant and full of tumult —

Where the Whales Are

I am going under the deep space —
      under the cost of things —
      below the dire abundance —

beneath the collective yes, beyond
      the gathered, absorbing now —
      into the blue emergence —

there, where the whales are, I am swimming
      in the open universe
      beyond this shorebound —

Journal Entry

I am broken tonight
with much giving, much being —
I long to close down
the windows and curl away
into the darkness where
the natural science of the moon
works like a salve
and the thousand eyes
the night has can see for me —
Fatigue bores in on me
with the weight of two or three lives,
lives I have lived,
and not sorted through —
so I turn to the high act,
the felt need of conscience
to face the demons —

to wash the burdens away
here, where the darkness swallows the pain —

To Be a Song

To be a song — this is my prayer —
to do more than just live —
I want to breathe in the scents,
here, in the country, woodsmoke,
some maple syrup, hotcakes,
and the coffee brewing,
I know I will be there, 5:30 A.M. at the diner —
I have had enough of pretensions —
let me stay awhile under the breezes,
let me rest my mind here,
where the ancient harmonies sing,
and like a bell, the mountains ring.

Stones in the River

I take these stones in the river
as prayer, as an intensity of devotion,
the climbing of mountains,
the decision to live, to be —

I work with the stones,
the essential meanings,
as the rejected stones of the builders,
as well as the marble of Italy,
the passing glances, the whims of mid-day —

of Christ + the rejected stone

The Cold of This Winter

In the deepening dark,
the wrap I wear is barely enough,
the cold of this winter,
closing in around me.
I sip my coffee in the darkness, then,
and feel the weight of the year.
The thousand wrong turnings,
a shaft towards death,
and this quiet voice on the other side
begins to sing, a song of welcome —

A Violette

Long into the endless night,
the delights and costs of Eden,
I taste in those hours,
and long into the endless night,
I give thee my love,
where the Rose of Sharon abides,
and flowers, flowers and then, the rose, come,
long into the endless night.

Midnight

Final things of the day —
letting go of a breath
as morning takes in —

outside — midnight —
pins of light all around me —
city lights — planes — stars — planets —

I reach into my pocket,
tossing a quarter into the dark — spinning sparks —
it realizes itself in my hand —

I stand there like a rod —
planted in the ground — a scepter —
a column in my family's building —

the night is food to me —
the air is a beverage —
bricks of the house are pylons for heaven —

I touch each artifact
in this present history — a blade of grass —
a sprig of mint — the wind is tipped with lemon —

Notes on Paradise

I

I am thinking of an absolute candidacy
for a piece of rope to swing by,
as a child gazes over a river,
there, from the bank,
in a wood where hobos are rumored to live —

II

I am thinking too, of a farm in Indiana
where three friends join forces
to raise grass-fed beef and organically grown
vegetables upon vegetables —
a make-shift solar greenhouse in fall,
a cow named Porscha to be warmth itself
and fill the refrigerator side wall with gallons
milk by milk, studies in human kindness,
three of them, reserving nap time, in the day,
reserving Friday nights for music and mulled cider —

III

The wildness of an Iowa Writer's Workshop type,
running a workshop on Martha's Vineyard,
wondering what ever happened to John Berryman,
Robert Lowell, and Robert Penn Warren,
as some college senior asks him about his work,
fielding the question, another question,
back to the poems at hand —

IV

Theory is an actuality
where you have the interview on tape,
and Afro-American Show number 9

will go down in a usual stellar way,
wording a line through Gwendolyn Brooks,
saving time for a question about whether poetry is
revolutionary —

V

Omnipresence is the beach
that is always there, off every continent,
transmuting, exploring itself with its waves,

finding its trans-original self
somewhere in the beach bum
who collides ever so casually with the mainstream —

VI

Agonistes is forgetting what you learned,
recognizing the same life-test coming,
rewinding the tape and nothing on it,
garbled, half-digested memories, life collapsing —

VII

Blessed be cucumbers, cool onion cream sauce,
    summer bravado at the beach,

O joy, to live in a hotel for the season,
 to swim the sauna, leaving the ocean
  for the ambitious and the foolish —

VIII

I indulge in a sweet avarice for food,
 a lightly seasoned gourmand,
  gourmet if pressed, but joy in the granary,
   joy in the amounts at the diner,
    wonder-songs for the wintered name of Christ
who sat down with the publicans and sinners,
   ate and drank and rebel-heart, really lived —

IX

Vision of loveliness, O planet,
 O dear Beauty,

  My Planet, My Planet, swing, you Orb,
  Be Thou Be!

X

I am thinking of a sainthood of immediacy,
 of Grahame Greene's term
  "the holiness of direct desire" —

I am thinking of the Buddhist monks who
        say "I eat when I eat and
        sleep when I sleep" —

I am thinking of an immersion in things
        in themselves,
so that living takes on an ethical electricity
        that is ground and vibrating atoms,
        source and reeling reach,
        find, continuum and change, Elysium —

Vision Quest

1

I am working the ground
as it stands — mind to world —
plowing, seeding, cultivate and harvest —
I am reading the world for my results,

it is my best catalogue —

2

I am sending myself elfin taking,
and saintly giving,
epicurean delights,
modern need, ancient remedies —

3

O singing, lift this voice,
lift its emblematic tenacity —

let it squire its verses,
let it breathe into its portents —

let speaking speak in this voice
let joy, delight, and consecration carry on here —

let my agonistes be bliss in its endings —
let my triumph be from the beginning —

4

Slender, tethered reed,
rise up and shout!

O granite slab, break forth into song!

Titan Sun, flare out in articulate flame!

O universe, give voice to your vision, there,
    in the eloquent cool dark, the ancient light,
        those critical cantankerous planets,
        those vision-moons, those vibrant stars!

O Divine, In-Dwelling, speak!

5

O unitary quest, bore down on borealis,
    for it is a bit of God's whimsy
    to have a light show, this aurora,
    brilliant as cinema,
    there on a northern big screen —

6

Questions, give me questions,
    for these are the "engines of intellectual inquiry"
  and the source of growing, let answers be few,
    and if found tethered, tested, sifted —

    let growing be in a context of situations known,
      felt through and won,
    driving toward the ultimate,
      facing the divine within,
    real-time jazzing to the new stream of the Tao
    conquering the down-side self,
      squaring up the ledger,
      going down the highway knowing true
        winning, true winning a success
    born of cosmos —

7

O ancients beyond, let me go vehemently toward the is —
let me drive myself toward my Beloved,

give the report of the next world in our thoughts,
    consume our anger,
content us with a muchness born of God,
    let plenty surround, let little be plenty,
    go far into us and let us go beyond beyond —

Shades of Violet

Violets, violets,
    I am seeing the world,
region by region, in shades of violet —

my Shenandoah summer
    lies violet and clipped,
like a fair vase in itself —

New England, cusp and apex,
    from Danbury to Kennebunk,
laughs awhile in these colors —

something Scandinavian,
    something sleepy and African,
I am thinking of gentle passions in violet —

A Poem of Friendship

I would see it this way —
that of all things gold,
and all things sterling,

a higher sort of friendship,
immersed in love or not,
this stands apart in mystery —

like the reasons of day,
or the logic of singing,
the fact of a friend, this is enough

to sway storms or seasons,
to settle continents
into a single town —

Autumn Luck

A feisty wind
with the autumn luck
to twirl a bit —

a leaf engages
in resolute drift,
conversing with the definite air —

The God of all seasons
tips the moment
with light rippling on burnt orange —

A New Rising

Advent, 1991

The spent husks
fall into a pile,

hugging the earth,
one by one, layered
like ruins —

on this rug of memory,
a new hope is prayed,
a new hinge is levered —

the old ache died well —
let a new thing rise, a royal falcon,
a bird of high resolve —

a new rising is shouldered —

The Day of the Buddha's Enlightenment

I

I am thinking of a day
in spring, when leaves
open out like hands —

when the union of trees
holds up the village —

2

Here, in my Shenandoah home,
I take time to go to the monastery,
the Buddhist monastery out Rt. 50 —

Sister Sama greets you —
reverential bows for Bhante Gee —

3

The lions roar less,
the last sub-species in the wild —
one-hundred forty species going down,

each day acid rain croaks on —
I lie in my bed of terror, 3 A.M. —

4

I think of Gary Snyder,
I think of Suzuki, Stephen Mitchell,
Merton, a wholly inebriate dove —

wonder-lover, the river
makes room for me to swim —

A Theory of History

The wicker morning
brought up a certain longing,
framing the world
on a mordant real,

forming the indelible world
on a windless afternoon,
there, on the Keys,
solving whole histories of religion
in a Confucian breath —

all this, while standing inside the circle
of a circle of a circle
of concentric villages
molding a reading sense of where
the first civilization lumbered into being —

High Hill Shining

Seat of the Universal House of Justice

In my solitary treading
up pilgrimage mount,
my wounded heart bursts —

what gorgeous marble white —
what lustre — what luminous —
this Universal House of Justice —

how history mends on these steps —
what high hill shining lit by night —
what consummate grace dreamed this dream —

Divine Lover

the loose-knit congregation,
here in the restaurant,
knowing something unknowable,
there in the mind

the divine sling we wear,
whispering a prayer
to the God who is larger
than our imaginations,
yet, will fit into a heart —

left standing there
at the end of a day,
uttering endless apologies
as winsome lovers,

who know their God as
Lover, Friend, Hero —
the uncommon hero who gives so much
you can't help wanting to say no —
then, turn around and wound yourself
saying yes a thousand times more
in return —

A Brief Theology

I am not sure of this, but
I venture this much — that God is
the reason for a sufficing terror —

one of the originals concerning
a "code for the road" — another name
for the unknown — a sworn mapping stone
for the way the human heart aches —
the chief object for the Druid curse,
by which to gain a blessing —
last hotel in the row for agnostics —
(sometimes the pleasure boat is full, or
doubt runs arid) — a quixotic way of looking
at the questions — an odd sort of answer
that refuses to let up — a chemistry
made of pride and humility — a ruinous gift
that wants all of you — a ruinous gift
that gives a great deal, if given —
once, possibly, someone who can't logically be
there, but is — the crux of things —
primal dark and primal light inebriant —
lodestone — crucible — find — source — river —

How Trees Vibrate

The trees vibrate today
with a lucid resonance —
there is something wholly adequate
about spring, today —

the main task for trees is to be —
being a tree, for them,
remains consummate wisdom —
it is a particularity for hard-boiled iconoclasts,
tough-minded realists, revolutionaries,

environmentalists, romantics, and
God-fearing Christians
who want to see a crucifix straight on —

above all, a tree, today,
makes ground by standing silent —
after all these centuries,
trees may mean something still —

Earned Tenderness

There lives an earned tenderness
in a yielding, regal heart —
in the richest loam of the gardener —
in the rabbi's cask of tears —

this is the farmed ache —
this is a blessing wrought of the curse —
here may be fruitage from the dark night of the soul —
this is a wine aged in a redolent crucible —

Oneness Wings

The whole inexorable flex
of the unfolding world Tao
triumphs on oneness wings —

the Bahá'í-Buddhist-Christian
swim resolves into a kind of delta
where river-life meshes into one ocean —

I am thinking of a place
where Buddhist monks and
Bahá'í teachers and agnostic seekers

can work with simple, sufficient tools
to build a cabin in the woods —
a place to face the big empty —

A Tincture of the Absolute

A tincture of the absolute
would be enough — a suggestion,

a limned, crescent moon
scoring the dark a bit —

a fold here, a tuck there
in the canvas of night

showing the way light bends —
the spectrum is not just one color —

nor is the way home single —
God may be kaleidoscopic —

To Wish One Thing

All the defiant wishes
dream down into one —
to merely and absolutely
be — to live thoroughly —

This is a triumphant giving —
    it knows time and timing —
    it nods to irony, obeys
    the higher laws and sings —

Being is not trapped by tarnish,
    but is impelled out and up
    into one whimsy and light —
    a single music and magnanimity —

Clarion

If there is a clarion day,
it is a trumpet to all living —

if we embrace, one to one,
then declamatory things follow —

when joys mount on joys,
then brass choirs enunciate —

when the God of all religions
rises on the horizon, singing,

then do trumpets sing, soaring —
then does Gabriel unfurl, with flourishes —

rise, rise, O ye dead, end your sorrow —
the joys of all the ages, speak it —

the Last Trump has sounded —
"arise, shine, your Light has come" —

Thanatos

The ageless is aged,
the giants are dwindled,
wholeness is whittled away —

thanatos, thanatos —

what leaves do not go —
what greatness is there,
when every tall tree is toppled?

thanatos, thanatos

Coltrane

Do you know how to sling the Harvard Divinity School,
    Tillich and Niebuhr, over your shoulder?
Do you know how to trade it all in going away,
    on a blade of grass?
Are you ready for Armageddon?
Do you know how to turn your back on its justice?
Is there rage in you you redeem in wildflowers?
Do you remember Coltrane?

Do you like to forget your telephone number?
Are you ready for dead-man walking in your own shoes?
Are you at home on the road?

Is there a way to nowhere, and can you return?

Is God a Friend, and is She your Mama, and is there
an Old Man in your Deity, and are you homeless?

Are your handles breaking, and do you see the world
new, fresh, endless, finally, on your knees?

In Memoriam

For Robert Hayden

A thousand sterling hours
cleft for the single gold —

so Robert Hayden wrote —
so he lived — unending good things,

set aside for the excellent —
yearning placed in a vase out of Keats —

what is the yesterday he felt
but the crucial yes after no —

Hayden knew how to say no —
he cut himself from his own fabric —

Hayden was in many ways his own invention —
yet he belongs to the world —

Robert, Robert, so I sing you —
hearing you have gone before us, singing —

The Seasons of Regret

In the seasons of regret,
I admonish myself,
exhort, drive, and claim —

still, do I relentless ache —
the fire in the belly roars on —
then, do I rise up beyond revolt —

into the sheerest risk
to feel at home, to accept
the tenderness I may have won,

by consolation or by shame,
by "fear and trembling" —
by endless consecrations —

The Uses of Art

What use art? A stretcher
to wheel in the wounded —

a monument of blossoms —
a bit of lattice work on the temple —

each painting, a record of a psychic diver —
each poem, an artefact —

life to be lived as a symphony, or
maybe just some chamber music for the few —

each breath, a brush stroke —
each day, a dance —

VIII

Waltzing with God

"We shall not cease from exploration
And the end of all our exploring
Will be to arrive where we started
And know the place for the first time."

T.S. Eliot

Waltzing with God

This wordless, whirling space,
where the "God beyond God" spends himself
herself, her, exactly, on you —

it is this precisely ancient present
where nothing need happen and
exactly everything does —

it is this crucial center
where roses are piled upon roses,
and she waltzes away with your wounds,

to give them to the wind,
where they are sung into amorous obloquies
which only you and she can hear —

Two Haiku
Cut in Glass

I jump on the train —
off to university
on two rails

I want to see behind my eyes —
blue-black pitch —
Isaiah's words spinning off my shadows —

First Light

I washed up, thrilling to the breaths
of water wishing away the brittle feeling

of solid night. I put on a denim shirt,
jeans, and my running shoes, a kind of loose
pact with myself that life itself
will not be unbearable. I wear what I choose
and toss on a sports jacket to face informality
with formality. Everything is in tandem,
clad in morning. Everything lives into the light shower,
even as frost glazes the apples.

Something Like Satisfaction

Sitting in the paneled basement,
legs crossed, on a couch,
(one of those new ones, rough cut,
plenty of wood to grab hold of),
drinking tomato juice with lemon,
3 A.M.

South Africa Demonstration

We find ourselves
out of ourselves;
we contain the pain of history
in the whispers of sweet nature,
here on the hill;
we think up into the stars;
we make moral tepidness
rise into a blue flame
of commitment.

An Introduction to the Humanities

The waitress at the diner
likes Barishnikov
and some of the Russian composers —
she particularly likes that finish
to the Firebird Suite
by Stravinsky —
a triumphant flourish
by trumpets —
she will watch the Nutcracker
for the nth time tonight —
(she likes the ballet,
and doesn't care for it on ice —)
she knows perfectly well
that she is sentimental
to think that Beethoven actually meant it
when he included the Schiller quote
on the Brotherhood of Man
in the Ode to Joy
of the 9th Symphony —

Cosmos at the Jefferson Memorial

I hear this longing
for reason
in the surrealism
of a jazzman
who wants to do classical —
or the loneliness

of the architect
who builds
a Parthenon
before our eyes.

Dogmatics at the Poetry Workshop

A leaf
kisses the branch good-by
then goes to work in the pond
for the rest of time.

Prayer

I glance at the stage
where I see my stage fright
and see two feet dancing there, still,
disembodied — I raise my voice
to the resistless hills,
disconsolate after the passing waves
of a purple yes — and hope that something
crimson will follow.

The Color Ivory

The meaning of ebony
is so simple,
so evident,
so elegant,
so perfect,

that only a teacher
would point it out —
just as the tree laughs
by the river.

Superrealist Painting

Hundreds of sparrows
fly overhead
as I drive into Charlottesville,
to visit Monticello.
I envision Mr. Jefferson
traveling to Moscow
to negotiate a
democracy of the world
some mid-summer soon.

Summit Song

The pas de deux
of these black doves,
flying their dance
over the readiness
of someone American,
of someone Russian,
to learn the idioms
of strangeness.

A Game of Poker

I ride the last riverboat
from Cincinnati
down the Mississippi
and tell this Chinese angel
that when Armageddon comes,
I hope to fly
with the Buddha
over the bow
into the fire
for the sake of peace.

The Attorney

The Virginia gentleman
rides his horse
back into the stable.
Then he sits down
at his mahogany mind
and writes the brief
adjudicating time —
it is a villanelle —
clearing the guilty .
and instructing the reader
in a reconstructive regimen
of roses in his private chamber.

Haiku

I mean by poetry
the things, the perfect things
that fly, that sing —

Another Song, Another Season

For Roger White

A song passes by,
a new song begins,
the music rises in its place,
and tugs at the air
like a mockingbird.
The play of it,
the delight in flying,
the swoop, the earned luck of soaring,
all, passes through our minds,
and we become —
ever so slightly more human —

The deafening fact
of our own arrivals —
crashing doors,
complaints, adjurations,
nothing quite right —
all this —
our groaning bones —

but the music, the music —

this, grows and grows,
without getting louder, or possibly
pleasing us with its crescendo —

by night, we are the people we see —
relaxed, to ourselves,
released from the day,
off to sleep,

and the music
carries us in the arms of God
into the brilliant sun,
a russet sky
at dawn,

where things resume and
music is the tender way we live —

Letter to God

For Roger White

Your High Majesty, Sire,
O Consequential, O Dire Abundance —
O Impelling Giver —

Your servant Roger,
Roger White, poet, friend,
wit, gallant, buckler

to the Bahá'í Revelation —
this Roger, the Roger of the bon mot,
Roger of the well-crafted poem,

he is no longer among us —
be well settled with him, Sire,
content yourself with his deeds —

confess him among your people —
make his name bright in paradise then,
conquer unhappiness with him,
make his radiance unending, as Eremite —

Old Moon

Old moon hangs on the sky evenings —
dawdles awhile at sunset —

keeps to himself mostly —
hides away daytimes —

but at the end of the month,
he comes out full to pay the bills —

A Surmise of Elegance

As we approached the Brown Palace Hotel,
a surmise of elegance
gained on my flying time to Denver —

the doorman held the solid brass door —
the bellman met me inside —
high tea was waiting —

a string quartet played Mozart —
momentarily, four-star dining within —
upstairs, the maid was turning down your bed —

Zero G's

I walked out over the edge
to see if the sky could fly,
leaning on a piece of cloud —
I loosened my tie,

                    then, lifted like a kite,
               learning the absolute bliss
               zero G's know how to give –
               nothing led to much nobody,
                    I settled into the same,
                    flying on my name –

Outside the In

          Outside the in,
          unusual up,
          Eden-type God,

          being the Him
          that He is on a whim –
          being the Her

          She is in the win
          it is to affirm, reckon and style,
          a slim-dancing all-around deity smile –

Dream Doctor

     The dream doctor is preparing a place
     where old sages come from,
     there where nobility lives,
     there, am I going –

     space between things will be enough there,
     time enough will be ours, for making,

sufficient food and lapidary days to spin dreams by,
gorgeous heart of God to know through the marrow —

The Edge of the Galaxy

I sing you
a certitude of earth,
in its plenitude —

its full-throated
well-singing floating
around the edge

of the galaxy, beyond
the vibrant center,
here, where the swell

of darksome space
ranges out in leagues,
fathoms to swim —

beyond, beyond,
our yearning missives
to the deep unknown, serve notice,
that we are here, and we are waiting —

Railroad Remembrance

I am dawdling awhile,
here, by the railroad tracks,

where a piece of earth
means more — history is definite

as a railroad tie — listening
for the engine is a way

to hear yourself — a casual waltz
with your friend down the tracks

surfaces old memories —
jumping a train at twelve —

the pullman car at four —
a rumbling sleeper to New York —

Good Old Sleep, Waking

Sleep rises from the aching bed
with a dream as large as being,
tucked away in memory,
there, where not even he goes —
something like an avalanche
opens out onto the day
and the old man sleep wakes into his dream,
some world of his, reading the world,
some definite heart of his,
feeling thoroughly, yes, there he is,
my friend sleep, talking,
taking his tea, his meals,
trumpeting something about Socrates,
enjoying Sartre at the deli,
good doable things like getting new tires,

or browsing at the bookstore,
and miracles in waking,
like touching the girl on her sleeve –

Zen and Groucho Marx

At the Amherst Diner
in Winchester, Virginia –
north on Rt. 81 –
I am nursing
a second cup of coffee.
I have beside me the poems
of an acquaintance of mine,
Gregory Orr, zen archer
in his own way – beside them,
the classic introduction to Zen
by Suzuki – my counter mate
and I miss Groucho –

Boardwalk at 1 A.M.

I am thinking of a minuet,
there, on the midnight beach,
cavorting with the wisps of day,
taking her by the arm, dancing,
down the perfect jazz it is
to do the boardwalk at 1 A.M. –
    I am thinking of a study
in a minor key – an etude –
this conundrum of the spent husks of life –
how the usual sand and surf

falls into a cool blue
on the dunes, where only we
rehearse the catalogue of waves
for some sand dollar or curl,
releasing the years themselves,
like a tumbling burden,
into the core image of open-eyed freedom,
the rolling dream that is summer —

Yessification

I went over the lip
of the century, in my mind —
I served a term there
debating vegetables and sausages
with the house cook — she
being in the perpendicular,
myself, in the right angle to a plane,
        we decided to move on
to horseradish, wherein we found
an enduring contentment, ensconced
just to the left of tabasco and hot mustard —
        this bit of dalliance
encouraged forays into hunan and szechuan,
which led us to yessification in mutual yum —

Lotus-Dancer

The crazed exotic dancer
whirrs in her precise whirl
into the eyes of the young men

where, like a dervish,
she stirs this mystic yearning
that only something so perfect as
a perfect fleshly form could satisfy —
her divine right almost, in giving so much,
so totally of her naked form,
invites a whole new category of yes —
that somehow the upbraided should upbraid
that somehow the unrighteous are slant righteous —
that Mary Magdalene lives on stage
even now, in some unfurling joy
as fresh and buxom as untold beauty —
this marigold, this flower, this dancer
learns things, she gives of herself,
she too is a kind of light —
her nude and nearly nude quest of desire
may well give the baptism of desire —
what lotus has not felt passion —

Something Celtic

An older form of being
draws down into my roots,
as if humans could be trees —

this incipient sense of dryad —
this village sense of bard —
this going home to Ireland —

I take my delight in dalliance —
I go to myself in my neighbor —
something Celtic afoot in Fitzgerald's heart —

Big Mama Blue Mania

I walloped the big one —
depression took the last train
out of Dodge — gone —

but, big mama blue mania,
she can stay — she's got my ticket —
she takes me places —

when we take a plane
to the West Coast,
the mountains salute —

we've paid enough dues by now —
coming into some real estate — meek enough —
going to write the check outright —

inherit the earth — inherit the earth —

If the Music is Dancing

If the music is dancing,
and the dancing is whirling,

then are the colors played out,
then do the songs sing themselves —

I am thinking of pure country days,
I am thinking of work held to the heart,

joys held close, then set free,
fountains of elaborate yes –

a highness wrought of song –
mountains as classical as jazz is jazz –

Handworks Gallery Vignette

Another free-flying
Handworks Gallery day –
Myrtis listens to African tunes –

Sallie shows an onyx ring –
Zulu baskets – Shenandoah Valley pottery –
kaleidoscope prisms bend the mind –

a friend sculpts coffee tables
out of sheer hunks of wood –
the day unfolds like its own river –

Searching for a Wife

In the mid-winter ache,
there at four A.M.,
right into the lexicon –

telling myself there's no one,
driving myself into a prayer,
heading it off, lest it happen,

something like four nights,
praying into it past where it was,
knowing it half-way open,

praying it down into the bars
for a year, two years, off with the coat,
paying for it, going nowhere,

my untended garden, yielding,
yielding swallowing me,
God, undeniable, lisping willows,

harrowed, into the train,
meeting her in baggage,
hugging, hugging, leaving, swirling, unending —

Used to Have a Life

The total lack of
        defines him — he is
the empty space over there —

there, where there used to be
        a house and children,
he dawdles over the shadow of

his car, making a leisurely way
        for his used to wife —
he is almost happy now, it is
        so exhilarating to
                nearly be —

Song of Wind

Every swim of the wind,
here in the mind, serves
the hearing of the actual —

for the wind is the echo
of what is — the river
sings the source of wind —

then, does living trace
the limned hope of God,
lassoing his own heart —

IX

Living the Tao

"The journey itself is home."

Basho

Living the Tao

In living the wide embrace
that is the Tao,
I am "dreaming a river",
sheer to its sources,
there, into its garnered heart,
its cosmic root
where the first tree grows —
this sits high on the Eden train,
yearns beyond yearning, and sees
as if seeing grass for the first time —
it is a serendipity of nocturnes and daylight
wound around the first and last,
sending itself the oceans of being —

Logos and the River

There is a view of logos,
that places it in lotus,
that places it in a tree,
that places it in the river —

I am going to watch a sunset,
how the sky is sprayed with
a roseate gloss, tossed like paint —
there is something perfect in everything —

Strands of Hope

In the ache the heart walks,
    I draw down
into the relentless love of God,
    forging myself

with strands of hope, gathered
    out of the dark,
into life force fire, giving—fire,
    love-fire, light of day —

I am content with no less than the river,
    for in the river I have
time and timelessness, intertwined —
    in the big Tao

I am Bahá'í — Buddhist — Sufi —
    I am Jew and I am Christian —
I build a lattice-work from strands of hope,
    and I "make it new" —

Lines to Myself

I'm going to wallet
a few memories today —
I am walking away
from the hurly-burly —

The old faces, the same
people, the whole fakery
of how things go down,
this, I will not miss —

but the real friends,
the real Tao, the Real —
the conclusive compassion —
I will take with me in yes —

what is missing is
the road and a love,
someone to tell it to —
so I got my legal pad friend,

settled in at the diner,
wrote these lines to myself —

Vortex of Thought

In the racing thoughts
at the end of the day, I lay
down the worst of it,

then, listen to the stream,
the steady pulse of thought
out from the culled risk —

for it is risk to live,
it is risk to think,
and it is a voracious day
that rests on the edge,
that cuts into the vortex
with each categorical breath —

It Is

On Bahá'í

It is somewhere in risk,
It is endlessly of the Tao,

It is finally consummation,
joy, delight, yearning of History —

It is quiet leaping of Islam,
part Christian, part Jewish,

It is a nod to the Buddha,
It is a close cousin of the Hindus —

It is a conforming tide
here, at the end of time,

It is its own ocean, It is,
It is, Source from the Source,
It is endlessly, endlessly river —

Idiot Expectation
and Puritan Particularity

A defensible rage
comes at the end
of articulate nails,

driven into the mind
and yelping heart
by idiot expectation —

vast pools of nobody's
business are needed —
copious nets full

of rascals should be
set loose on the puerile
who run the circus —

all of us poor monkeys
should be set free
to roam the woods,

foisting Puritan particularity
on the highest tree
to sour in the wind,
explode, and disappear at last —

Heart-Drawn Roses

Sweet dozens of roses,
sweet thousands of scents,
the rose of relentless giving,
attar of comfort, attar of joy,

abundant laughter roses,
surety of dynamic cohesion,
Universal House, seat of the harness,

riding the horses to the roses,
Church of the Big Blue Dome,
sky-walking, far into the night,

'Abdu'l-Bahá, the Master, scouring
the last ruination of the spent soul,

my wounds laid open, my heart-drawn
tender-walking lady friend, my sweet roses,
from my thousands of broken moments, I give you,
roses —

Religion

Crushing rose petals underfoot,
Prince Buddha
rises into the ether leaving a tree —

Les Philosophes

Here is Erasmus
and here is Kant,
writing world federalism

several centuries before
the United Nations Charter —

Lyricism
and the Philosophers

One thinks of Shelley or Keats
with the word lyricism — however,
I am thinking of the German Kant,
just beginning to write as he retires —

Plato or Aristotle — pure guides —
lamp–posts — end points and starters —
mapmakers of the mind — a way home —
favorites of 'Abdu'l-Bahá, the Master —

then, I think again, of John Rawls —
the Harvard philosopher — writing
so well about justice and matters of right —
something wry, something warm-hearted in it —

Dewey or James — practical men
with spiritual intent — *tous rois* —

A Brief Ontology

I am thinking of Jurgen Habermas
and the neo-Hegelians with their
critique of domination — Derrida
and the Deconstructionists — endlessly pointing to what is not —

taking joy in a single leaf that is —

A Memory At Evening

In the altitudes of evening,
I gravitate toward some hewn wood,
here, in my studio, where
memory is engraved in grains

made of softwood — I remember
seeing you in spring, there,
wrapped in the L.L. Bean bag —
your legs poking out like fun —

I will never recover somehow
that you are not here now, my dear —

Wishing on You,
Tucking Myself into
a Convenient Constellation

Leaning into the slip-stream
        night is at 2 A.M.,
I delegate my dreams to a star,
        then, tucking myself
into a convenient constellation,
        I shore up my chances
by wishing on you — I cannot regret
        that it is someone who
is quietly the best of the best —
crème de la crème,
la même — a screamingly outstanding
        example of the Creator
at his play — yourself, a wish for
        joy-beauty-beaming acceptance,
like the final dream — delight —

Fighting the Beastie

Fighting the beastie —
maybe to be Zen Baptist —

not more courage, but
more melting ability —

maybe to say "alchemy" —
or "mocha nut fudge" —

fighting beastie woo
means not to fight, but

to hug the ghosted hauntie —
to smile — to snicker —

for the beastie can't stand it
when you know, too —

persistence is your best weapon —
feeling a bit fogged in?

mind on hold — take a peek —
beastie woo is peeking, too —

The Friendship of Night

O night, night, you and I
sit here, in my chamber,
3 A.M. and a song playing —

the lamp shines too loudly,
as some might say, and God is
feeling a bit cagey toward us —

then, break out the bread,
break out some cheese, and be
a friend to me with your wine —

Taking the Eden Train

I hurled myself
into it, 4 A.M.,
hard at it, gone,
into the swing,
driving real-time,
hugging the ache,
holding the blue space,
socking myself for it,
driving the nail on it,
holding into the be,
riding the river to Eden,
taking that Eden train,
seeing the new day roar,
going on home to Buddha,
singing my sweet Jesus,
road-dogging, 'til Sunday,
on down to the riverside
hotel where I get free,
whole hum longing 'til morning —

Dreaming Well

At the center of the Tao,
there works a deeper river.
This together-heart steps up

into the outlandish grace
it is to dream well.

Out of all dreaming and days,
the Tao draws down, deep,
into its own waters, and swims —
then, is the Tao consoled, there,
in the perfect crush of its own living —

You/you/you

For my brother

You are a his and hers blues specialist
you have expertise in the Way of Zen —

you have historic meetings with your mind in the restaurant
you travel to a New England town meeting on the ocean's
    coast —

you talk on the phone like a dolphin
you ride the train into the future, your own porter —

you are beautiful, your Irish folk songs are beautiful
you like high tech, low tech, inside-outside days —

you watch an Andes year go by and find your find
you/you/you/ — you live like cajuns, like gypsies —

you dance the dance on the common ground,
you fly to the West Coast or Kyoto, watching the wing
disappear —

Searching the Interior

I

I am searching the interior
for signs of the absolute, searching
that terrain where being is a wisp of mind,
vibrating with the tensile lift
ideas bring to the casual conversation —

II

I am scanning the landscape I am
to scour it out, to scrub it,
to fully inure it to its pain,
so the work and worth of loving will be
toward the clear resonance of itself —

III

The verve of it, the vigor,
this vivacious living in the Tao,
the way of life common to all religions,
this is the Tao that is not limited, but open,
each idea, a piece of grass, surrounded by grass —

IV

Vernal equation, O spring, come,
make your mathematics, your equalities
between spring and violets,
between the month of May and carnations,
O splendid June, be my Roses, my sweet attar —

V

O complexity, bow a bit, blend a bit,
confer simple things where things are simple,
defer to eloquent elemental things,
combine thyself with the earthly basics,
sinewy, simple, not simplistic, O elegant be!

VI

O how often do I pass my days in the diner,
or the pizza parlor or the tavern,
sipping, paying, swooning a bit over the lack of alcohol,
yet bonded to the people of my town, this Shenandoah town,
like some elfin creature, some prayer meant to be with them —

VII

Someday soon, I will dive again,
into the inner depths, driving myself down,
swirling there, among the spiritual choral creatures,
the coral along the edge, up and out,
onto my own inner terrain, so California, so totally not —

VIII

The inner journey is a tether to the safe world above,
there where things are normal, conventional, middle class,
yet, I am going down, into the brooding be —
I am heading down, into the sober breakers
where conscious life takes shape —

IX

I am organizing my square inch of earth,
I am giving my tendrils of earth-thought,
I am giving my ten dollars, so friends,
remember me as I remember you,
let us, then, come through for each other —

O powers of earth and heaven,
be with my friends as they go,
let them travel in safe convivial ranks,
let them squire their monies, let them speak peaceably,
let joy-springs attend their days, unending —

Shenandoah Quartet

I

Shenandoah sweet Shenandoah sweet,
sing in me, O tired, tried, blue wonder —
sing in me of your past-dark past your soul-self
sing me, O Valley, O River, your trident,
this weary soul is driving on for the south,
some other part of you, like Shenandoah Self #3,
or Shenandoah Self #6, #7, where I am taking in
the bold average, the vibrant blue real —

II

O victory, that a war was won here,
ending injustice, as the south ended injustice
by bleeding over it, wrong-headed, nonetheless
dual partners in a purging, blood brothers,
sworn to slaying death, sworn to risking wounds,
all to unhinge the practical sense, untenable
that some non-union committed to slavery
and freedom, at the same time, that fiction,

could endure — O fiction that God was blind
to oppression, O fiction that God did not care
about all the soldiers, unsung, unfit to battle,
even as human beings are not meant for murder —

III

My friends own these shops here,
and even if I do say so, they are very fine —
elegance, charm, grace, abound —
sprightly, vibrant women, men, youth,
making springtime somehow year round —
O foolish heart, speak these praises and know
that someone somewhere is cackling about
some fool poet who loves a home, a poet who
lives towards his town, even on the road,
a someone who is so innocent he refuses
to acknowledge the aggravated evils of a place —
let these pass away — let us address them —
undo the hurt — undo the injustice —
but let us temper our lives and the coming
generations with a gentle past —

IV

O foibles, O wonder heart,
what comes of a man who listens to his heart,
who yearns from the bottoms of his worn shoes
for the single thing he has,
who lives out of the back of his car almost,
yet knows a fine hotel,
suspires for fine classical music,

unfolds his lyre for the wealthy,
considers that joy was made in these hills,
knows an unending passion for travel,
yet also, for these tender mountains,
these confident trees,
these configured towns,
these blessed mornings, there, at the diner,
praying lightly under his breath to the God
who made a tempered land out of these scenes,
these hill-songs where nature finds herself
singing, singing, singing —

Incarnational Theology

For Ronald Santoni

My friend, Ron, founding member
of Philosophers for Peace,
speaks in Jerusalem
against holocaust and genocide
(preventive medicine for infectious war) —
later that evening, Ron and friends
sample some olives — five or six kinds —
in the Arab quarter — falafel for dinner —
a walk around Old Jerusalem with a Jew,
a Christian Humanist, a Native American,
a Russian, and a Chinese Buddhist —

Japanese Studies

My friend,
a Japanese potter,

told me one day
that pottery
was 10% technique
and 90% philosophy —
He works with mugs
the person can fit
their thumb into
like a lap — but
the most important part
is the fire.

Tunnel

A tunnel to roses
is the story I am reporting;

A by-way
for useful people;

A history of time
in transition and

a bolt of lightning
on a clear day —

the cost of reason or
the reason of insight are my themes —

a single strand of hair
is the meaning —

and a line
in the highway is the face in the window —

Couplet

The Einstein equation isn't really it –
it is the sheer elegance behind it –

Color Chart

I am thinking of mocha,
    a well-blended brown,
I am thinking of a cool tan,
    there in the heart of fleshtone –
Give me a russet beach scene,
    and I will have high-kicking affirmations –

Interior Research

I want to research
the interior savannah,

the *favaleh* in the mind –
those Elysian fields within –

somehow, the cerebral cortex
must be part Eden –

somehow, as Michael Ryan might say:
"There must be God-hunger in the brain" –

A White Stone

This semiotic fusion I live
merges brick, fieldstone and woodsmoke
into its own wholeness.
Beyond the sensate vigor
of one being set off against another,
I choose the "Yes!" of earth,
fire and ice, restive, compassionate lines
made of listening rest
to walk into the corporate nest.
I speak of the love of
things in themselves,
like the image of the real —
a farmhouse with the pine outside
by the road, yielding in its height
to the acreage behind.
I take this charge as
the silence of history,
impelled into history's music
I choose this fieldstone way
as the heart's call to
the mirrored white stone of overcoming.

Pastorale

On seeing a shaft of light,
everything is a cord of wood,
stacked on the porch,
plenty of hard wood,
for a long, even burn.

Confessional

I rescued the ruins for myself —
I have saved the wreckage out —
life's brutal crush abates for now —
the gale winds out to sea —
the beaches, strewn with torn and articulate artifacts
recommend themselves — researcher,
go out to these labors, then,
more than I can say, building
some marker, some sculpture from the salvage —
take the gaping ships, the tossed driftwood,
bury the bodies, and with all due ceremony —
then, send the banshee back, and
give out the news of coming weather —

Excavation

I repelled down
the side of my mind,
then dug in the place I found —

this led to
the most natural order
ribbed by its own interior law of
Deos found —

the excavation dug itself —
the lights down deep
formed a code of survival
heaped up with a country wrung out of its terror —

theology becomes lapidary —
whole eras of unseeing
collapsed into the stones
and God settled among us like Orion's dust —

A Handful of Certitudes

I am sure of it, more
than the wind, more than ivory,
more than road-time and more
than the fact of getting there,

that doing the Tao
lives in the bones of us,
that sin is there for forgiveness,
that redemption needs our mistakes —

so I am going into the mind,
that nexus of heart and spirit,
yes, and my old perplexities sum down
to a handful of certitudes,

followed by humming days on the river,
at home with doubt, at home with knowing —

Haiku

Peace roars
at the hotel earth —
everyday miracles of bliss —

A Silo of Unspoken Hopes

I resurrect like a prayer
from an afternoon bed
where the day is disappearing
into a silo of unspoken hopes —

the wash of nighttime agonistes
lies dormant, complete for now —
day will be a sieve
by which I funnel off disaster —

a Corsican blue hope rises —
an olive-skinned woman strolls into view —
I will create a new order
out of mosaic tile,
and remember olive trees in Jerusalem —

The Deep Room

A total window on the actual —
so is the husbanded earth —
a broken heart fully plowed —
           this summary dream —
           a consonant rest —
yet how does the heart see, of itself —
how then, does the feeling break —
where is the deep room
where all the ruined lives mend —

Sifting Spider Talk

In the first place, I am not
a spider — I am arachne —
mere moralism does not suit me —
matters of conscience for me
yes, these are developmental —
here, elegance, beauty, grace devolve —
moral imperatives draw out into webs,
wrought out by edicts made of strands —
ethics are clearly circular —
my motive force is lattice —
my world is not merely moral but ethos —
spinning is a matter of aesthetics —
do not come only to dine — I am daggered —
be powerful — do not seek stasis —
drive me, destroy me — and I am grateful —
new webs grow out of downed ones —
I do not like mere country idylls —
entertain my dear, do not dawdle —
begone, if you do not conquer me —
at all ods bodkins joy — delight me —
caveat emptor — my world is singular —
sift my meaning — visit if you are strong —

A Hunch of Magnitudes

Tonight, I am drafting the plan
for a lake which I will lay out
in the mind — the water is
            from a river
I draw off from the unfathomed yes —

I yearn toward it like a turning wheel,
reeling from it within a hunch of magnitudes —

The Crucial Questions
Lean on Laughter

What cold lock on things
melts a bit with whimsy —
what spent heart
heals a bit with a dance —

the crucial questions
lean on laughter —
solemnity lives toward
the logic of its own release —

God releases us, I think,
from the chains of our making
when our gift explodes
with outlandish, roaring gratitude —

A Feast of Losses

For Stanley Kunitz

"A feast of losses"
was our rude food
one night on the edge

when the main course
was the food of memory
grown from a dry ache —

it was a gruel
and a satisfaction
that was truly our own —

you own your losses —
and the rest is expectation —
such food is fuel

for the prayers of the broken-hearted —
these petitions need no words —
God is close companion to such tears —

As If Solid Dread Could Dream

As if solid dread could dream,
    as if wholeness were magmatic,
    I draw down into the core —

Through sheer heft of breakage,
    the worst of things falls to ruins —
    the risk of actual goodness surprises —

Something beyond control or polish —
    the weight of authenticity —
    the husks of real living —

A Music Sounding at the Core

A lucid resonance
forms in the mind
a sense of the Source —

sonority and roundness
sculpting in sound,
giving a way home —

life becomes somehow lyric,
the whole of the text
becomes a music sounding at the core —

Meditation

How to sum up, here,
Sunday morning, mid-winter —
then, isn't the divine an ache —
isn't it a way home —

would a single sparrow be
enough? Is a meditation
on a single leaf about right?
Are we already there?

A Strand of Current

In the extremity
of a single strand
of current, the eye
spirals down in reflex,
bearing witness to it,
testifying of current,
meandering itself, a bit,
as the convex river ropes,
twirls, becoming concave,

187

surmounting only snapshot-self,
becoming more in the perpendiculars
we set up for ourselves
to compare visions of what we saw,
like glints of light, here and gone,
our hearts, twirling too,
in the pressing need to see,
to see straight on, to see whole,
accurately, precisely, strong —

The Right Anger of a River

The right anger of a river,
driving into its current,
swells and tosses with personhood —

she is — he is — sufficient, roaring —
it is as if a woman rolled her back,
toppling all traffic — hurling

the idea of indignation into time —

Bahá'í-Buddhist-Christian Rivers

Past all the angers,
past the unusual hatred,
under the bridges of being,

there lives a wideness,
largeness, a plenitude,
sufficient and bold,

there, an embrace rimmed for loving,
in all the rooms of the Tao,
Bahá'í-Buddhist-Christian rivers, unending —

To Think Awhile

I relent from doing
to solely think awhile —

thinking dwells down
into the rivers within,

forming a well—spring
made of a country idyll —

then, my heart will soar,
winging on the hard-won

actual of the mind's home,
a thought, a wisp of prayer —

Mid-Winter Ride

Into the whip and rush
of a drive down the Valley,
post-midnight, mid-winter —

I think of Stonewall and his men —
the ride down the Valley —
thirsty for it — the madness of it all —

driving by New Market —
passing a clotch of eighteen-wheelers —
thinking of the New Market cadets —

hungry for the road —
snow blasting the wind-shield,
ripping the window open anyway —

night-walking, up energy —
mind-flying down the throat of the Valley —
searching for a new way to do Tao —

X

Dreaming a River

"The intellect is an eternal gift."

'Abdu'l-Bahá

Dreaming a River

I am dreaming a river
of the real beyond the real,
that place beyond borders –

I am going to the river of all rivers,
the river in the mind
where Jordan, Ganges and Yangtse come from –

I am going to the place where I am comes from
to the sense of the lateral vision
that the world is rising up from its sources,

that the world is dreaming itself,
so no prior thing need be assumed or not assumed,
all is contained within our wholeness, dreaming –

A Friend's Farm

Sharon and Arthur order a cord
of mixed soft and hard wood,
mostly hard for a slow burn,
and we lean into the cold evening
like sparrows.

Sharon has some new herb remedies
and the moon is nearly full.
We chart a course for the world
or baby Duncan,
breath following breath,

Eden on our brows
like incense
or the cost of our food —

forty-five cents each
for a pack of
cucumber, tomato or lettuce seeds last spring,
lights in the coop for a year,
enough stone and corn
to feed the chickens
long enough to lay a dozen eggs,
potatoes from potatoes from potatoes.

If She Were My Trident

If she were my trident,
I would relentless walk,
waking through the hours,

steady my heart, she is
the heart-won, she is the real,
she is the summary verse —

this joy-song in human flesh,
she is the home you are seeking,
she is quiet, longing, and leaping —

Road-Cut Life

Inert images of a gradient icon,
these road-cuts surface in the encrusted mind,

like cousins of stalagmite unities.
A layer at a time, since pre-history,
limestone selves, dust off the side
of a primordial river, compacted
like anapests. I drive to an old haunt,
Thunder Cove, Maine, near Bar Harbor,
or a Blue Ridge roadside and slate,
moving into shale, slides
into the portals of the imagination.
This is a mica-joy, a reflection in strata,
a purple amethyst life, crushed open,
struck in the very questions that form
certainties out of interior heat and pressure.
I hunch down over a fire in the granite dark,
and take my tectonic dreams
into the cave where Rt. 70 becomes
old National Road, I lose
the wagons west, and sift through cro-magnon dust.
Quartz reliance on an absolute zero day
resolves into my arctic longing
in the evolutionary pool, and I disappear
into a region beyond baselines, beyond geologists
and shift into Mesozoic life in a current
as broad, as particular as stones.

Sheaves of Tears

If there are tears, undoing
the hem of living,
the wheat may say the hope.
When the tears
come in sheaves, though

and reaping is
a crest of blue showers,
then, thinking is a solace,
as direct as
the yellow sun and
the green lake.
Reasons for living,
rising again in the fresh morning,
resolve in the aching flesh and
the body becomes its own dew.

Treaty

I sipped my coffee at the diner today,
here, in the Shenandoah Valley,
seventy miles outside Washington, DC.
An odd grey light over the Valley,
luminous, mild, forgiving –
reminded me of a photograph of the Soviet tundra
I had seen at the age of nine.

Canaveral Couplets

A miracle of light mounted the sky
with its jets, a propulsion liberty

wrought out of steel. A cathedral of fire,
this angel of warning, this limb of the whole of man,

climbed the millenia of history.
It caromed into and beyond

gravity's grasp, and sound broke.
A complex of mind and metal

bent its course toward the purple planets.
A myriad constancies came into play

as instruments made emptiness redolent
and the merest bit of darkness became

the discovery of habitable space.

At the Third Level Out
From Hell

At the third level out from hell,
I saw the goose-steppers coming on,
so I wailed on my road-dogging,

threw myself into the world-circle,
chopped a few Vermont logs,
walloped my heart with some sun-tea,

then, forded the stream between there,
yes, there and the very concept of Vermont,
living until the end of hotels in the new era suite.

Inner Tyrant

There is a graceless god,
dictator of custom, unblamed

guilt-purveyor, riveting us
to our needless shame –

this is the satan of shoulds –
this is the unbidden detector –
this is the relentless, nameless
unction that nails you until

you give up what you earned –
this is how you fall into it,
the soup that soaks you in custom,
endive fashion that demands an apology

for every act, no matter how kind,
how close to the bone, how exact –
this is the tyrant who stands in
where the real God waits, mercy, shining –

Nightingales and Roses

Ridván
April 21 – May 2

Ridván, paradise, home –
in spring, situate on an island,
prisoner, house arrest, nonetheless,
then, Baha'u'llah declared
His Liberations, His new freedom –

in that place, slavery broke
its insolvent back – equality

made magnum progress — roses,
nightingales and joy broke forth
amid a roaring justice —

this was a particular grace
of a Spirit-King — this, the giant
munificence of a High Prophet —
to free women in a single breath —
to watch it unfold is history —

Three Women, Three Virginias

Three women, three Virginias
in my family, circle in delightsome
gifts to the world — Grandmother
Jinny, spelled with a "J",
adjunct pastor as minister's wife —
counselor, mediator, editorial
assistant for sermons — warm
as sun-showers, baskets of love
for the world — sister Jinny,
astute doctor, diagnoses that save
lives, mezzo-soprano of first-class
calibre, warm and bright as chestnuts —
cousin Jinny, teacher, mother, wife,
Unitarian, dancer — young professional
with no apologies herself — fun-loving
lover of Maine — each, a modern woman,
tough-tender, warm like bathing water,
   bright as the need of the time, and more,
   these resonant women who live musically —

An Evening Performance

At the evening performance,
the trumpet player, first chair,

settled his embouchure with a glass
of water, then a handkerchief,

glanced briefly at the audience,
the house full, dressed to the nines,

leaving no doubt to the rising
portals of sound as the brass quintet

left the earth with Fanfare for the Common Man,
Copland etching phrases of eternal yes,

across the evening and across the century,
making the word clarion brand new.

Vignette in Blue

A jazzman lights up
outside the old pizza parlor,
first cigarette in a week,
culling his thoughts for a tune,
settling in with his memories,
humming a riff
from an old standard,
nothing left to dream, but
dreaming itself —
going down to the river,

some day soon,
going down to the joy-song river —

Diner Days

Endless refills
on 6 A.M. cups of coffee
for the ham-fisted men at the counter —

waitresses straight out of the depression
with names like Frankie, Thelma Lou
Doris and Dee Dee —

sausage gravy, scrapple,
home fries, and morning papers —
businessmen running business from a booth —

The Graces of the Deity

The love of God is
like a wonderful melon
you open up like morning —

the graces of the Deity
are this freshness on the wind,
an evening cool off Cape Cod —

God may be this fragrance,
possibly a touch of lemon,
with a sprig of mint —

Some Things Matter

Some things matter —
I am listening to Bonnie Raitt
under a southern moon —

a local blues band, later,
has a harmonica man going
real strong —

and the radical priest
had lunch with me today —
he's helping a refugee —

my old man has retired —
he's watching Nolan Ryan
stay fast at forty-five —

the Jesuit says "Om Jesu"
I quiet myself at Yom Kippur,
and say "Om Yahweh, Om Dhamma",

my sister, the doctor,
saved an Hispanic kid's life,
and mama is tired —

Appalachian Reasons

I am thinking of the cost of perfection
and the wind of music itself;
the long drive down the Skyline Drive

is an opening to deer and Big Meadows,
far enough along the Appalachians
to see brownness in its place and
to clip the sound of finches
from the trees with your witness.

Something Like This

I am listening to a country song,
in a pizza place in the Valley.
It is the Valley to those who know it.
The Shenandoah Valley to the tourist bureau
and the chambers of commerce.
It is the scenic Shenandoah Valley
with its scenic overlooks and
its scenic by-ways to those who live by cliches
like "succulent snapper" and "zesty marinara sauce".
Still, it is our place, we live here,
and have learned its value as a base,
as a way to reach Washington and New York
in a day and leave them behind, too.
I find my conversations with people
last longer here and the country song
shows me the leisure of spaces between things.
I rest closer to my inner life at night
by being somehow shaded from
the insolence of power in D.C. or
the uproarious, livid dream of New York,
day in and day out. The needs of
spiritual life take on the dimensions of
a shared cup of coffee at the diner or
a full hour at the cafe.

The striking thing about this median grade
up a hill toward death is its
kinship to a song, and I take the time
to see my mother as she is.
Somewhat shy, a child still in many ways,
a hug, someone to talk about art with,
someone to see the Valley with, and take time with
to say "It is so hard. It is so beautiful."

Two Bright Moons

For the Rubes

Omniscient God, your son David
    surely is an emblem
of knowing — for his knowledge
    encompasses sciences,
policy, theology, art, and the heart of man —
    as his dear wife Margaret
still gives out lovely blossoms in age,
    So David is for the ages —
the two of them are surely "two bright moons" —
    they know Israel — they know you —
theirs is an earthly concourse of heaven —
    when high honour is passed
around like a cup of choice wine,
    they will not be passed by —
nor will they taste only lightly —
    for they have drunk deep
in advance, knowing the table of their Lord,
    knowing service as honor,
informed loving as means and end,
    lofty aim, and a high hill —

Gabriel Has Taken Wing

For Dizzy Gillespie

Gabriel has taken wing —
a horn so plentiful and full,
full of the pyrotechnics of love —

an ecstatic re-invention of Eden —
fundamentals turned to spirals
of sound trumpeting joy —

today, center stage is deep
with an empty space as large
as history will allow —

Be-Bop is left without currents of memory —
the horizon of jazz is dimmed —
America, the world, and the Bahá'ís

wait to hear heaven blow —
we have stardust to reckon with —
Louis has company now —
Dizzy has gone to join the saints —

The Impossible Garden of Eden

I would rather see a cardinal
and I would rather live in a dream,
than tie myself to a tether —

I would rather take my bread and cheese
at the restaurant or café
than miss my highs and lows —

I will be out on the road for longer
than I will be studying in the city
so give me a country sky —

show me the lessons of the grass
and instruct me in the ways of the river
and I will take instruction well —

show me the mountains and show me
the impossible garden of Eden —
and I will comfort myself
by the banks of the Shenandoah —

Sea Shanty

I am sailing myself,
by the average maybe,
going nowhere but yes,
after everything goes,
seeing myself as clipper,
being no more the schooner,
just cutting a cutter,
nobody more than special —
so I am who I be I am —
extra bit of nobody aboard —
quiet then, I'll send one up
for old Kentuck — one for NYC —
get your prayers in now —
we're heading out to sea —

You Are the Rivers

My dear, I want to look at you
from every angle — as my palace —
a hermitage — a plan among plans —

you are the sheerest giving —
you are the rivers — the poems —
you surmount a surfeit of pain —

you are the sufficing love —
you transform the totally average —
you remake a cup of tea into the worlds of God —